THE ART OF IMPERFECT HEALING

Also by Sheila Bridge

The Art of Plate Spinning

The Art of Imperfect Parenting

Hope for the Hard-pressed Parent

Sheila Bridge

Hodder & Stoughton
LONDON SYDNEY AUCKLAND

British Library Cataloguing in Publication Data
A record for this book is available from the British Library

ISBN 0 340 62134 6

Typeset by Hewer Text Composition Services, Edinburgh
Printed and bound in Great Britain by
Clays Ltd, St Ives plc

Hodder and Stoughton Ltd
A division of Hodder Headline PLC
338 Euston Road
London NW1 3BH

To David, Emma and Matthew,
who have to live with my imperfections;
with my love and prayers.

Contents

Foreword

If only, if only, if only I had read this book a few years ago. Some kind friend could have given it to me as a Christmas present shortly after our first child had arrived and altered my life forever.

The timing would have been ideal. Over the Christmas holiday, I could have realised why I was so crabby and bad tempered. The broken nights, the absorption of my wife's attentions, the anxiety over the welfare of a tiny life that was my responsibility – all would have been explained. I could have been easier to live with. I might have been a better parent all these years. I'm sure I would have been saved countless hours of heartache and brain strain as I grappled with the most important task I have ever been given – being a parent. If only.

Our three children are all grown up now. They have actually turned out wonderfully and I am proud of each of them. I am pleased to say that it is a fortunate thing that we all have a heavenly Father capable of overruling our blunders and being a much better parent to our children than we could ever be.

The thing I discovered was so profoundly different about this book is that it isn't just another book on how to be a better parent. It is refreshingly different in addressing the deepfelt needs of a parent as a person. During twenty-five years parenting I have been through ecstasies of pride in my "successes" and deep depressions at my "failures". I have experienced immense fulfilment when my children told me they appreciated me and dreadful disappointment when they ignored my advice and did their own thing. I set out with high hopes of creating a family so happy, caring and peace-loving that all other Christian families world wide might have an example to follow. My dream suffered a bit of a setback when my subconscious persuaded my conscious mind to recognise that I was regularly shouting at the children and the day I threw a telephone directory at one of them in anger finally forced me to abandon the dream for reality.

I went through such a gamut of mixed up, confused feelings. Now I know quite a lot more of what I was experiencing and why. Sheila has revealed all. She understands how us parents feel and how to grow up to be a relatively sane and happy parent. I think she has an unusual gift in identifying the strange workings of the human parenting psyche and expressing herself clearly, readably and colourfully.

I love her humour, her chatty style and her bright analytical mind. She takes the living God as her guide and the Bible as her guide book but is not too heavenly minded to help us earthy parents.

I have one other very good reason for commending this book. Sheila recently became my sister-in-law. With her husband David and their two children, my wife and I have felt privileged to have our family enriched. I can therefore tell you that this book comes out of the genuine experience of a Christian family, written with honesty and integrity. I believe God will use this quietly powerful book to touch the lives of thousands of individuals, struggling to stay upright on the banana skin of parenthood.

Max Sinclair
Sevenoaks, Kent

Introduction

The experience of being a parent has often been compared to the experience of riding a roller-coaster. One moment you're on top of the world and the view's great and in the next moment you feel like you are plummeting towards disaster. However, unlike those on the fairground ride, parents are not allowed to shut their eyes until this experience is all over. Instead they have to continually make split-second decisions that will affect the outcome of the ride.

Let me show you what I mean by describing a typical early morning scene that could take place in any household. Maybe it happened at your house this morning? Your school-age child decides that she doesn't want to go to school today and would like 'peace and quiet' in her own room without her younger brother. She sets about achieving 'peace and quiet' by literally booting her poor unsuspecting brother out of the room. Not surprisingly this leads to an indignant, wailing, younger child calling 'foul' and demanding intervention from Mum or Dad. The arrival of a parent on the scene causes the older child to wax loud and lyrical about her rights to 'peace and quiet' although she can hardly be heard above the lung power of her brother. There follows much mayhem; slammed doors, stomping, grumping and thumping. Meanwhile the clock is ticking away the time you have left before setting off to school.

You have only just got out of bed and suddenly you are judge, jury, prosecutor and defender all rolled into one. You are angry because your daughter's behaviour is so unreasonable and belligerent. You are worried; is she ill? Has something upset her at school? Is she just tired? You also feel guilty because, if she does need to stay at home, you don't know if you can stand the company of a stomping six-year old all day. You make a quick decision; yes, she is fit for school and even if she would benefit from a day at home you can't be seen to reward this bad behaviour. With the decision made all that remains is for you to persuade the foul-tempered, stubborn child into her clothes, through her breakfast and out the door. No small task. Little wonder then, that when she turns into 'instant sunshine' at the sight of a friend in the playground, you collapse into a blubbering heap. I hope you had a sympathetic friend near by!

It is very difficult to cope with the whole range of emotions swimming around our brains at the best of times, let alone first thing in the morning. At such times being a parent can feel like an overwhelming task: so many decisions and so little peace in which to think them through. Often when we do sit and think it's just to go over where we've gone wrong or what we should have done better or even to think how much better everyone else seems to be doing.

This book is for anyone who has ever felt like that, 'hard-pressed on every side' as Paul put it in 2 Corinthians 4:8. It is not going to tell you about your child, how he develops, what he needs or how he feels. It is not even going to give you much advice on how to change him. Instead it's all about you: what you need, how you feel, how you can stay sane and how you can change so that you can actually enjoy parenthood in spite of being a normal, failing human being.

With so much emphasis on the importance of the family

from the media and in politics we can feel a great deal of pressure to 'get it right'. So much so that when we see our normal children exhibiting normal bad behaviour we have a tendency to panic and despair and feel it's all going wrong. The purpose of this book is to encourage you. Not to tell you how to be the 'perfect parent' but to allow you to make peace with your imperfections.

Before I am misunderstood let me just say that making peace with your imperfections does not mean that we should be content with our failings or not try to be the best parents we can be. However, I do feel that unless we honestly face up to the negative feelings that parenthood can at times cause in us we cannot best decide how to go on and cope in spite of them. Sometimes we *are* angry, we *do* worry, we *do* feel crushed by guilt and a sense of failure. Understanding why we feel this way and knowing how to handle ourselves at such times can go a long way towards making us happier and probably better parents.

In my bid to tell it like it is, I have used the pronouns 'he' and 'she' at random. I apologise if this is confusing but in my experience children do come randomly in 'he's and 'she's and they are frequently confusing little beings.

THE THEORY

CHAPTER ONE

Why 'Imperfect Parenting'?

Have you ever tried to master some new skill? Maybe you've tried your hand at embroidery or DIY? Or perhaps it was fishing or learning a new language? Full of enthusiasm and determination you've set out to enrol for a class or started collecting one of those helpful magazines that builds into a 'complete manual in fifty-two weekly parts'. You expect that with a little time and effort you ought to be able to master this new skill. You'd be surprised and maybe a little affronted, if when you got to the college, you found it offered courses in 'Careless Cross-stitch' or 'Bad Plumbing for Beginners'. I doubt you'd sign on! Nor would you be likely to buy a magazine entitled 'The Incomplete Angler' or 'Easy French in Five and Half Years'. So why have you picked up a book entitled 'The Art of Imperfect Parenting'? Of all the skills or vocations isn't *this* the one you'd most like to get right?

Sure you'd like to get it right, don't we all? We'd all like to be a loving and lovable, wise and witty 'ideal parent'. Someone with the gentle wisdom of Bill Cosby, the dedication of Mother Teresa, the imagination of Steven Spielberg, all blended with a little honest simplicity and a pinch of humility. We may have set out on the adventure of parenting with that kind of ideal in mind but it doesn't take long to discover that we do not need tuition in how to be an imperfect parent, it comes to us quite naturally. What we do need to learn is how to handle our disappointment with ourselves and our families; we are less than perfect and so are they. This is the 'art' with which this book concerns itself: not how to be imperfect, but how to be the best you can be, in spite of your imperfections.

Just as 'Easy French in Five and a Half Years' is a more realistic title for a course of study, so I hope that this book will take a realistic approach to the whole subject of parenting. I am not promising you any neat set formulas that will instantly make you an excellent parent because this is not a skill that can be learned quickly, not in five and a half years, not in ten or twenty. No matter how much time and effort you put in, even a lifetime of learning will not make you into an all-wise and all-knowing parent. Far from disheartening us, this fact should help us see the value of coming to terms now with our imperfections.

The emphasis in this book is going to be on the only person in your family who you can directly influence and affect: you. The reason for this is not because you are the person most to blame but rather it is because no matter how much you'd like to change your child's aggressive behaviour or your teenager's indifference or your spouse's uncooperative attitude, it is not in your power to do so. The decision to change their behaviour is one that only they can make, you cannot decide for them that they are going to change. Only they can make that choice, just as you are the only one who can take responsibility for a change in your attitude and response to their behaviour. So if you have picked up this book with a particular problem in mind – perhaps your child is defiant and arrogant and you are looking for advice on how to change his attitude – there are any number of other books on the family life shelf that attempt to tell you how to do that. This book will mostly concern itself with changing *your* behaviour and if you are willing to consider that as an option you may well find it is the most effective place to start.

Instead of waiting around for your child to change, you can, with God's help, begin today to change your attitude and response in a way that might alter the whole picture. I am not suggesting you change your behaviour because you are wholly to blame for whatever your problem happens to be; not at all. I'm suggesting you change because you are the only person for whom you can take the responsibility to change.

One of the most frustrating things about parenting is that it is a skill we have to learn 'on the job'. We don't usually get to practise on other people's children first nor can any amount of Parentcraft classes prepare us for the reality. I was chatting with a friend over some small dilemma she was facing to do with her son and she remarked, 'It's the uncertainty I can't stand; if someone would just say "this is what you should do" then I'd go and do it confidently.'

We often joke, don't we, about the arrival of our first child, 'if only it came with a full set of instructions'. The fact is that because every child and every situation is different there are an immense number of variables that affect all the small decisions parents have to make: the child's age, temperament, the amount of time the parent has available, the rest of the family's needs. There are so many variables that no one could ever issue a neat set of fool-proof instructions for successful child-rearing. The best we can hope for are guidelines based on our beliefs and values but each family has to then interpret such guidelines in a way that is appropriate for their family.

REAL QUESTIONS AND DIFFICULT FEELINGS

As my friend noted, this 'learning as you go' process makes for a lot of anxiety. Anxiety often leads to confusion and guilt: 'What is the right way to bring up my kids?', 'What if I've been doing it all wrong?', 'What if I'm messing up their lives?' These are very real questions that most of us consign to the nagging worry department of our mind because, after all, 'we can only do our best' and most of us sincerely attempt to do just that most of the time. No matter how much we try to avoid these inner doubts, we are all made to face them at some time, usually at the very worst times. For it is life's big events, especially the painful ones, which bring us face to face with our fears and anxieties.

The birth of our first child is the overwhelming event that launches us into parenthood. Shortly after my first child was born, someone said to me that the experience of guilt is like an unseen bundle delivered with your baby. The bundle idea only partially describes what parental guilt feels like: it's heavy and it gets in the way but you could always stuff a bundle away at the back of a cupboard. But guilt is only one of the negative feelings that came into your life in a new way when you had a child, the others being anger and anxiety, or feelings related to these. I find it helpful to picture these negative feelings as a trio of little dogs. (Dog lovers, forgive me.) These are not a pampered trio of parlour pets: Pansy, Posy and Poppet. No, these little hounds from hell are more likely to be called Snappy, Yappy and Grabbit. Like little dogs, these feelings constantly 'yap' for attention, just when you are trying to get on with the job, to make a decision or to sort out a problem, there they are at your feet, tripping you up and yapping so loudly that you can't think straight.

There are three things you could do with these troublesome pets: 1) You could ignore them. 2) You could feed them. 3) You could face up to them squarely and put them in their place.

IGNORE THEM

At first glance, option one sounds like a wise choice and it is certainly a popular one. Taking this option tends to produce the sort of parent for whom being in control is very important. They tend to be strict, well-organised and efficient (although it does not follow that everyone who is well-organised and efficient is denying their feelings). Their family is run around a fairly rigid framework of rules, they are somewhat inflexible and feel very uncomfortable with uncertainties or problems that appear to have no obvious solution. If you were to compare them to pilots, they like to fly with their hands firmly on the controls. Faced with any dilemma, they might say something like, 'Let's just make sensible choices about how to bring up our kids and stick to them'. This sounds reasonable enough and sometimes it might be the only thing that can be said. But if you identify yourself with these parents and if that is the only thing you ever say when you are troubled by these feelings that cause you confusion, it may be that you are missing out on hearing something important about your parenting style. Allowing guilt, anxiety and confusion to be heard is the equivalent of allowing ourselves to admit we might be wrong.

FEED THEM

What if you take option two? This means feeding, patting, stroking and becoming totally preoccupied with your fears and worries. The result of taking this option will be that you will feel overwhelmed. If you were a pilot it could be said that you are flying by the seat of your pants! You may feel so disheartened that any attempt to improve as a parent may seem too daunting: 'I can't help the way I am, maybe I've already made a mess of it, I daren't try a different approach in case I fail.' This is the point of view of a discouraged parent; it is very understandable given the stressful lives we lead and given that there is so much conflicting advice and so much pressure from society at large, a society that expects us to make the best possible job of parenting in an ever worsening social climate. When the odds seem stacked against us making even a half-way decent job of parenting we can feel like giving up. I can sympathise with this point of view but I wouldn't be doing you much good if I just patted your fears and said, 'Well, yes, that's what life is like and we're all imperfect so don't hope for too much.' You might feel understood but you'd still be left with all your worry and guilt.

FACE THEM

I would like us to take the third option with these three troublesome dogs. Facing them squarely and putting them firmly in their place is the equivalent of looking carefully at the kind of parent I am, of asking myself, what situations cause me real anxiety or concern? When do I feel guilty? What is it that makes me afraid? To use the pilot analogy again, this type of parent would be seeking to use the controls as skilfully as they could whilst being constantly aware of the prevailing weather conditions that threaten to blow them off course and away from their destination. Once we are more fully aware of our fears, confusions and guilt then we are better able to assess, 'How much of this guilt do I really deserve?', 'Which of my fears are unreasonable?', 'What confusions am I unable to resolve?' and finally 'How would I like to change?'

Option three would be pointless if there were nothing constructive to do with the results of our assessment. The good news is that when we are left with the guilt we know we deserve but can't get rid of, the fears we know we can't handle and the questions we can't answer, God has something to offer. He offers forgiveness for all the things we wish we'd done differently and his unending, unconditional love, a love that answers our fears by saying, 'nothing can separate you from my love for you' (Romans 8:39). He offers wisdom to all who ask for it and a handbook for living in his word, the Bible.

The whole of this book is devoted to option three. In the next chapter we are going to have a good look at ourselves and face up to the guilt, anxiety or fears that we have as parents. In chapters three, four and five we are going to take a good look at God and begin to see how tapping into his supply of love and forgiveness for us can help us to be the best we can be. The second half of the book looks at three specific problem areas where the supply of God's love can make all the difference.

None of this is intended as a 'fool-proof guide to parenting in three easy steps'; all that is offered is a way of thinking about ourselves and about God that is based on biblical truths, and suggestions arising from these truths that have been 'fired in the furnace' of ordinary family life.

CHAPTER TWO

Squaring Up

Here is a gentle opening question to begin this process of squaring up to our inner feelings: what surprised you the most about becoming a parent? Was it the amount of paraphernalia required to care for one small being? Was it the way time began to slip through your fingers before you'd done anything with it? Or was it the discovery that doubling your numbers with your second child made four times the work?

The thing that most surprised me about being a parent, was me! Some nice surprises about myself, about the love I was capable of feeling, about the tasks I found I could do that had seemed previously impossible. So far so good, but there were also some unpleasant surprises in store. I'd like to tell you about a time when I made two unwelcome discoveries about myself.

THE BAD NEWS

The first unwelcome discovery was made in a very ordinary children's play park which happened to be very crowded on that particular Sunday afternoon. Gran and I had decided to take the children out for some fresh air and exercise. My daughter, Emma, was just over two and very confident on swings and slides. She ran off excitedly on to a huge piece of play equipment. Her younger brother, in his pram, was grizzling a bit and needed to sleep. I only looked down for a moment to settle him with his soother but in that brief moment Emma had vanished.

As we were amongst so many other children we didn't panic at first, we simply scanned through all the arms and legs on the climbing frame looking for the right pair of shoes or her brightly coloured sun-hat.

'I can't see her, can you? She must be here somewhere.'

Leaving Gran with the pram I went round to the other side of the play area, aware that my pulse was rising and telling myself that her cheeky little face would appear at any moment. I circled round again, past Gran who gave an anxious shake of her head. On the third time round I lost my inhibitions and started to call her name frantically. I hadn't noticed it earlier but in the front of the play area there was a lake, behind it was a wood. In my mind's eye I could see policemen dragging the former and thrashing through the latter. What was she wearing today? Did I have a recent photo of her?

We decided to split up. Gran widened the search to include another play area about one hundred yards away, I was finding it harder and harder to keep a lid on the rising panic and anxiety within me. In all it can't have been more than ten minutes before Gran reappeared with Emma in tow, but it had felt like forever. The relief was almost as overwhelming as the fear had been. We collapsed in a heap of tears and hugs over a blissfully unaware child and I don't think I stopped shaking until my third cup of tea.

I had made discovery number one: I am limited in my capabilities. This incident really brought this fact alive for me in a way nothing else could have done. We often joke about needing 'eyes in the back of our heads' but the simple fact is we don't have them; we are not all-seeing, all-knowing and all-powerful. While I was searching for

Emma my feelings of love for her were so immense and my desire to protect her was so desperate but neither of these feelings made one ounce of difference in the face of my own complete helplessness; no matter how much I loved her, I could not help her, I could not rescue her, I could not even find her.

It's fairly typical of all of us that we depend the most fervently on God when we are in the biggest trouble and I was no exception to this. As I searched I remember repeating over and over again, 'I don't know where she is, Lord, but you do, you can see her.' It was rather more a statement of fact than a request but it reflected the fact that when I was most painfully aware of my inability to find her I depended the most on God's ability to see her. Only when I could see how fragile was the fence of protection I thought I'd put around her did I trust more deeply in God's protection of her. I thought I was capable of keeping her safe but I realised that I am, in fact, extremely limited in my ability to do that. When I own up to my limits I'm more likely to trust God.

What does this mean? That if we deepen our trust in God we are free to let our children wander off? Should we abandon stair-gates and cycle-helmets because 'God will keep them safe'? Not at all. We are called to be responsible parents and it is entirely good that we take every reasonable measure to keep our children safe, but if we take this entire responsibility into our own hands without taking into account our own limitations we are setting ourselves an impossible task. We cannot always be on hand for our kids – we do not have the resources or the answers. It is when we bump into these limitations that God wants us to trust him.

Is he trustworthy? What if Emma really had been abducted? Would my trust in God have been misplaced? Many parents have faced just this situation, but most of us only face the fear of it. We'll look at the whole issue of 'Is God trustworthy?' in a later chapter on anxiety; for the time being let's just get hold of the fact that it is God's desire for us that we depend on his ability and we cannot do this fully until we recognise our inability.

THE VERY BAD NEWS

Discovery number two was made on a very mundane Monday afternoon, a mere twenty-four hours after the 'discovery' in the park. It had been a typically busy morning, dishes to wash, clothes to hang out, children to feed, dress and entertain. I was very glad when we got to midday and I could send Emma up for her afternoon nap: this meant I could at last settle down and give Matthew his first peaceful feed of the day. I had persevered with feeding him myself but it was a wonder we'd both survived the nine short weeks of his life as feeding did not appear to be his favourite pastime – screaming was! A successful feed required complete concentration from me and no distractions for him. After the usual ten-minute struggle to get him successfully settled into a steady rhythm of sucking, I was just breathing a sigh of relief when Emma reappeared . . . nappyless.

The sight of an untrained child without a nappy at any time amounts to a severe disturbance of the peace but as if her untimely and unaided trip downstairs weren't enough, she remarked, 'My nappy was dirty, I took it off for Mummy'. (She was a very articulate toddler.)

Somehow I just knew that her attempts at disposal would require gallons of hot water and lashings of disinfectant and I was right. The sight and smell of her bedroom, the mess in the bathroom and the sound of Matthew returning to his preferred pastime all combined in me to blow a fuse. I 'flipped my lid', 'threw a wobbly', 'ranted and raved': in short I lost my temper. It was probably a good thing that there was a good deal of scrubbing to do, on which I could take out my anger, but I did also do a fair amount of ranting, most of which was undeserved. The poor child had, after all, only been trying to help.

Eventually it was all sorted out, Matthew was fed, my daughter slept, the place was cleaned up. It took me much longer to calm down inside. The strength of my irrational anger had really shocked me. I'm not pretending for a moment that this was the first, nor would it be the last time that I lost my temper, but this particular occasion really shook me because it contrasted so strongly with how I had felt the day before in the park. How was it possible to feel so tender, so loving and protective on one day and within twenty-four hours feel so angry, frustrated and irritated by the very same child? I felt like I was riding on an emotional roller-coaster. At one moment feeling the heights of love and protectiveness and the next plunging into anger and frustration. It didn't seem right somehow, but that is what life is like for parents.

It also disturbed me that children don't need to go out of their way to make us angry. They can provoke it by simply being children and doing childish things. I admit there were mitigating circumstances when I blew my fuse; I was tired, harassed and fraught. These factors don't constitute a defence but they do make my outburst more understandable. Understandable or not, what shocked me was how powerless I was to stop the flood of this violent emotion pouring out over the head of my daughter. If I could feel this angry when she didn't deserve it, what hope did I have of responding calmly when she did?

In this way I made discovery number two: I am flawed in my character. There is a huge gap between how I am as a parent and how I'd like to be. The fact is that God knows about this gap and would like to fill it. He'd like to make up for the times I've failed my kids, by wrapping them in his love, healing the hurts I've unintentionally inflicted, building up the bruised egos that I've blundered into. Clearly this is an ongoing process in my children's lives and also in my life. The way to start that process now is by learning to depend on him, learning to accept his understanding and forgiveness for my failures and learning to rely on him to help me with my shortcomings.

LEARNING TO DEPEND ON SOMEONE ELSE

This learning process is central to the 'art of imperfect parenting'. It is a depending, relying and accepting process that can all be summed up in one word: trust. I must learn to trust, call on and take comfort from my Heavenly Father. In short, I have to learn to depend on him just like my young children depend on me. I need to learn that he does understand and care for me even though it doesn't always feel that way.

In a society that considers self-sufficiency to be a desirable personal attribute, anyone who is leaning or depending on someone else because they are aware of their own flaws and limitations is seen as weak and inadequate. Anyone caught leaning on God must be seriously inadequate! Many Christian parents anxious not to associate themselves with the idea that God is a prop for 'weak people' have gone too far the other way as far as independence and self-reliance are concerned. When it comes to a task like parenting in which they want to 'succeed', they trust themselves more than they trust God. By their own efforts such as reading books or going to seminars, they hope to equip themselves with the resources to get this task right, but they overlook *the* only resource, God himself.

Let me hastily add that there is nothing wrong with going on courses or reading books to improve your skills as a parent, but if your reason for doing so is based on the assumption that following all the good advice will automatically guarantee you the outcome of a stable and happy home, then there is a fundamental flaw in your thinking. The flaw lies in the fact that all your effort is based on self-reliance. It is likely that effort will bring some results but if it doesn't then you are left feeling guilty or a failure because 'you must have gone wrong somewhere'. It follows that if all the responsibility lies with you then so must all the blame.

I've met people whose lives and attitudes express this very sentiment; they are godly, devoted parents whose children are a credit to them (that usually means at least two in full-time Christian service!). Quite unconsciously their lives express the attitude that if we diligently follow all the advice then we will have the 'perfect Christian home'. I also know plenty of other parents equally diligent and caring whose children are not like that; their children may have abandoned a Christian lifestyle. How might these people feel when they meet the first set of people? In a word, 'guilty'. They might wonder, 'Where did we go wrong?' Who knows? Maybe they *did* go wrong at some points but possibly no more so than the first group of 'successful' parents. Both the 'successful' and 'unsuccessful' parents have swallowed whole the assumption that 'it was possible for them to get it right' and in so doing have overlooked the facts: *a*) it was only possible for them to get some things right, some of the time and *b*) part of the responsibility for how children turn out lies with the children themselves, or to put it theologically, children have free will.

If we look at God as an example of parenthood, surely he is the perfect parent. He doesn't have the limitations and flaws that we have. How then do we explain all the trouble he had with the children of Israel? Did he go wrong somewhere? No. All that their rebelliousness tells us is that they had free will, as do our children. Unlike the children of Israel, however, our children do not have perfect parents; we will get things wrong because we are flawed and limited individuals, we cannot afford to rely on ourselves. God calls us to depend on him but, as we shall see, he does not offer any guarantee that doing so will result in the 'successful' family we'd like.

We have to give up this unrealistic and harmful notion that we can get parenting 'right' so long as we know the right formula to use or the right way to pray. Apart from being dangerously self-reliant, it demonstrates a conditional response to God. God is not a formula, he is a personal being who wants to make himself known to us through the whole of life. The trouble is, we are more interested in what he can do for us to improve life than we are in getting to know him for himself. Thus we prefer to hold God in some sort of mental 'half-nelson' position ('If I do such and such, God, then will you make such and such happen?') that would offer us a guarantee that our families will turn out well. We prefer to hold God in this wrestling position rather than begin the scary process of knowing him better and trusting him, whatever happens.

The fact that God does not offer us the sort of guarantee we'd like to have should not dissuade us from developing dependency upon him. If we realistically take into account the facts: our children have free will, and we are limited in our capabilities and flawed in our characters, then we will realise more than ever our need to depend on an infinite and loving God.

FROM SELF-RELIANCE TO GOD-RELIANCE

It only takes the average number of children a few weeks of conspiring in their average normal way (endless broken nights, tantrums three times a day, that sort of thing) to totally disorganise family life, to unravel their parents' patience and to have them signing up to join the ranks of overwhelmed parents. If these poor parents believed that 'they ought to have been able to do this', they will feel terrible failures. In fact they should be allowed to feel relief – who expected them to have all the resources necessary for parenthood? Society may have, but God never expected that of them. His desire and expectation is only that we hand over our limited resources into his hands, like the boy with the loaves and the fishes, and trust him for the rest.

The first step in learning to depend on God is discovering where you need help. I joined the ranks of overwhelmed parents at about the same time that I made the two discoveries I've described. If you're only just joining me, take heart, there's a lot of us here! Don't be afraid to join us and admit that you too are an imperfect parent. This sounds a rather easy thing to ask you to do; most of us would not be so arrogant as to suggest that we were perfect parents. However, what I'm suggesting isn't quite as easy as it first sounds. You see I'm not just asking you to admit you are imperfect but to square up with exactly how you are imperfect.

This does not sound like an agreeable thing to do – you may even feel it sounds unproductive and unpleasant. I agree it may be uncomfortable but it will be useful. Our need to feel in control, our tendency for self-reliance and a strong sense that we 'ought' to be able to do this, all conspire to ensure that we do not rely on God. Dependence on God does not come naturally, we have to be shown our need of it and this is a process we do not enjoy. This uncomfortable process is the stuff of the next chapter. It is a necessary process because only when we are fully aware of our worries, fears, failings, joys, hopes and dreams can we place the whole lot totally into our Heavenly Father's hands. It is a hopeful process full of the promise that God is the one who redeems and transforms sinful people and bad situations. He is the God who multiplies the little we have and delights to work with ordinary fallible human beings.

CHAPTER THREE

The Problem Is Me

I like to think of myself as a 'pretty well put together' sort of person. It flatters me when other people see me as an unflustered and competent mother. I've even been guilty of trying to ensure they do see me that way: the trouble is I keep getting caught out.

Too many people have witnessed my usual late arrival at the school gate and overheard such terse parting remarks as 'You'll have to bring your dinner money tomorrow' or 'Stop whining! I'm sure your reading book will dry out over the radiator'. None of these witnesses would ever believe all is efficient calm in our house over breakfast. Too many people have seen me in a wound-up worried heap over some new venture, to ever believe that I sail through life fearlessly. Too often have I been seen leaving church fit to burst with irritation at the two small 'fidget fiends' I took with me. No one watching me worship God with one child climbing over my head and the other sinking both hands into my pockets, would ever believe that I am whole-heartedly enjoying the experience.

I think all of us try our best to look our best, most of the time, for the best of reasons. After all, there's nothing to be gained by giving full rein to our annoyance, impatience or fear in every public place. Exposure, if it's going to happen, is usually best with just one or two good friends on hand to witness your fall from 'perfection'. Close friends knew you weren't 'well put together' anyway and they accept you the way you are. The trouble comes when we don't allow ourselves to lower our guard, even with close friends; then we are at risk of running a serious cover-up operation.

A COVER-UP OPERATION

We finished the last chapter saying that the necessary first step in the process of learning to depend on God was to face up to our shortcomings and imperfections and to try and understand why we are the way we are. Our tendency is to cover up our bad moments and negative feelings.

Just how dangerous this covering up can be was vividly pictured for me a little while ago on a shopping trip. I had to go to a toy shop in another town to buy a large item. I managed to find the shop even though I only had a rough idea where it was in the precinct. It had a beautiful bright display of toys in the window, games and teddies piled high, dolls' houses and little trains running between toy stations. Inside the well-lit shop were neat arrangements of toy cars, piles of fireman's helmets, rows of puzzles and stacks of boxes of all shapes and sizes. There were helpful signs telling me which aisle displayed the toys suitable for which age group. The staff were friendly and available to help me make my choice. So far so good and just as you'd expect. I paid for my item and as it was rather too large for me to carry away, I enquired about collecting it from the back of the shop.

'No problem, madam. Just bring your car up to the back door, present us with the receipt and we'll hand it out to you.'

When I got round to the back of the shop it was quite a different story. I had a job to work out which back door belonged to which shop and when I did finally see the small toy shop sign I found I couldn't park up close enough anyway. The steel-plated back door was in a dark unlit porch up some steps that were strewn with rubbish. When my eyes had adjusted to the gloom, I found the bell was so high up I could only just reach it. With some relief, I pressed it, hoping to be soon out of such an unsavoury place. I waited . . . and waited . . . and waited. Nobody came. I rang again and again, and after about five minutes I gave up ringing and started knocking. After another five minutes knocking gave way to kicking. (I reasoned it was a long way for the sound of knocking to carry but I confess I found kicking much more satisfying.) Time was running out, I'd have to repark the car in order to go all the way round to the front of the shop and there wouldn't be time to do that and make it back for my daughter coming out of school. Finally after a quarter of an hour spent stomping and thumping the door opened and a young shop assistant said,

'Oh, I'm so sorry. I didn't know you were there. I think the bell must be broken.'

As I drove home I thought to myself, 'Some people's lives are like that shop. All bright and well-organised on the public front, but desolate, despairing and firmly shut at the back door.' As I thought about it some more the inevitable personal conviction settled in on me, 'Never mind about other people, sometimes *my* life is like that.' I know I have been guilty of only letting people see the 'shiny shop goods': a patient manner with the children, a tolerance for noisy play, an enthusiasm for their 'music'. Am I only happy to welcome people into the shop-front where all is well-lit and swept clean? Well, it's understandable. The trouble comes when that is also the only place I'm willing to welcome Jesus, because He's round at the back door among the discarded boxes and neglected rubbish of my life, ringing the bell for all he's worth. Am I listening? Have I disconnected the bell box?

In other words, are there parts of our lives that we'd rather not face? Maybe a difficult relationship, perhaps an unloving attitude or an ingrained pattern of responding judgementally to others. Maybe it's an explosive temper or moodiness that we've lived with for so long we tolerate it as 'just the way I am'. Or it could be a critical tongue that always seems to put down rather than praise.

Maybe also 'round the back' stored well away from God's reach, are a pile of hurts or disappointments that we feel are best ignored, if only they would stop tripping us up. These hurts might go back to childhood or they may relate to your marriage partner, or even to the place where you live. God cannot come in and clean up the back of your shop until you are willing to own up to all these hurts and ingrained habits, in other words to face the mess honestly together.

What I am talking about is owning up to God and maybe a few close friends, not the sort of 'let it all hang out' honesty that is urged upon us by some Christians whose 'honest sharing' is in fact a pursuit of acceptance from others in a 'Here I am warts and all' fashion. This attitude is unhelpful and it is not usually accompanied by a commitment to change and grow. Jesus is interested in change; honesty is just part of the process. He does not require us to tell everyone about how our kid drives us barmy because to do so would be disrespectful to our kid and rather than spurring anyone else on to being patient and loving, it would simply allow them to think, 'Well, I can't be so bad'. Such a negative emotion is best shared with God and a small circle of close friends: we were not made to withstand self-exposure on a massive scale. God desires that we be honest about our failings, but his purpose is to change us. He doesn't want us to simply feel more at home with our shortcomings just because they seem to be casually accepted by our friends. God is interested in cleaning up our whole shop, in making the back door look more and more like the front, in changing us so that how we are on the outside is a closer reflection of how we are inside.

Another factor holding our cover-up operation in place may be fear. The fear that once we admit we are weak in one area – maybe we are short-tempered or over-anxious – God will point out the other flaws in our character. This fear is justified. He will do this, but he will do it gently, 'a bruised reed he will not break' (Isaiah 42:3). As we are honest with him about our shortcomings there is no condemnation in his reply but there is no let-up either. The reason why he relentlessly points out our weakness is that the more clearly we see our need of him, the more likely we are to depend on him and the more adequately he is able to meet our needs. There is no point covering up in front of God, especially as children are some of the best tools he has for undermining our self-sufficient, ordered lives. They can scramble our brains through lack of sleep, destroy our dignity through their defiant behaviour and tie us in knots of anxiety as we watch them charge out innocently to tangle with life.

CLOSING THE GAPS

The change that God wants to make in us is to close the gap between how we are as parents and how we'd like to be. If you've never noticed this gap maybe these situations will show you what I mean. Imagine you've had guests to tea, they've lingered a little too long and the children have been getting 'wild' while your attention has been taken up with your guests. You may be smiling at your guests and dealing calmly and patiently with the children. Now move on in time, what is the scene like five minutes after your visitors leave? 'Get up those stairs, now!' 'Turn that racket off!' . . . How big is the difference?

The presence of outside observers isn't always required to show up this gap: your child is in a bad mood, he is very irritable and short-tempered and you know it may be because he has been hurt or upset at school. Even though you know this and you also know that what your child most needs is more positive, loving input from you, he is so unpleasant and abrupt that you cannot bring yourself to spend any time with him. You may even get annoyed if you try 'It isn't my fault you're upset', 'There's no need to be so touchy', 'If you're going to behave like that why should I care'.

Finally: it's a bright, sunny Saturday and you've been doing chores all morning. After lunch you just get to sit down and junior asks you to play a game of football. You know you've been fobbing him off all morning, you know it's a reasonable, polite request but somehow the paper and your cup of coffee are so much more appealing.

I'm not saying that parents don't ever deserve time to themselves, nor that we should never leave a bad-tempered child alone in order for him to calm down. What I am saying is does the coffee and paper win every time? Do we remember to make time to repair the relationship with the grumpy child once the temper has passed? Or are we so grateful it's over that we'd rather not go back over it for the necessary repair and restoration?

I've made these examples slightly extreme to demonstrate the fact that sometimes when we know what we should do as parents we don't have the desire to do it. Even if we have the desire sometimes we don't have the power. No one has summed this up better than Paul in his letter to the Romans when he said, 'For I have the desire to do what is good, but I cannot carry it out. For what I do is not the good I want to do; no, the evil I do not want to do – this I keep on doing' (Romans 7: 18, 19).

So what is it that causes the gap between how we are and how we'd like to be? Paul goes on to tell us the answer to this question in the same passage. He says, in v 20, that it is 'sin living in me'. 'Sin' can sound like a rather a vague notion, but if we start to talk about self-centredness, greed, competitiveness, impatience, and lack of compassion it all starts to sound rather more familiar.

Remember that we should be relying on God's help to clean up our shop, front and back, not on our own self-effort. What is needed is not a resolution such as 'I must not make sarcastic remarks' but a clean sweep that uncovers, 'Why is it that I make sarcastic remarks to my kids anyway?' It may also be worth reminding you at this point that God isn't out to haul us over the coals for one 'bad day' with our children; one hurtful remark, one outburst or one act of care that we neglected because we were so exhausted from lack of sleep. God isn't in the business of keeping a record of wrongs. He understands our 'bad days'. I'm not talking about changing these occasional shortcomings, I'm saying let's take a step back from ourselves and take a look at the things we consistently find hard and know we struggle with every day. Is it a nagging anxiety we can't help passing on to our kids? Is it an inability to really show love and tenderness, or an inability to praise and to encourage, unconditionally? It is these things, these effects of sin that God wants to change in us by his power.

Christian psychologist Larry Crabb in his book *Inside Out*[1] has helpfully pointed out that we are affected by sin in two ways: we are agents of sin and we are victims of sin. Being agents of sin means simply that we are sinners, we commit sin. We are, at times, demanding, unreasonable, unfair and unloving towards our fellow human beings. We are responsible for these sinful ways of behaving. When we are guilty we have to own up to the fact of our guilt and rely again and again on God's promise that 'if we confess our sins he is faithful and just and will cleanse us from all unrighteousness' (1 John 1:9).

Also as 'agents of sin' we are like pawns in the much larger battle between good and evil that is going on in the world. The forces of evil are on a mission to destroy homes and families, to spoil relationships and wreak havoc in society. Some Christians speak more of an awareness of Satan in this battle than an awareness of their own sinfulness. It might amount to much the same thing, but beware the 'pet demon' theory that says 'our family is the way it is because it is being attacked by the forces of evil in this world'. While it *is* undoubtedly true that Satan is actively undermining and oppressing every family, it is also true that he can safely leave us to cause many of our own problems all by ourselves as a result of our lack of discipline and our selfishness. I should like to caution against any way of thinking that is a subtle abdication of responsibility for our sin, in other words whenever we are tempted to say, 'it wasn't me, it was my pet demon', we should examine ourselves carefully. We are responsible for our own actions and choices, to do good or to do evil. We will not win every battle and it is consoling to remember that there are few places where the battle is hotter than in our families but that thought must not cause us to give up. When we do lose a battle we can have confidence in the power of repentance and the reality of God's forgiveness.

So if sin is the cause of this gap between how we are and how we'd like to be, why do we sin? Part of the answer to this question lies in what I've just said: we are inherently sinful people – but another part of the answer is that we sin because we have been sinned against; in other words we are 'victims of sin'. The sins of others have scarred and damaged us over the years and we have developed sinful ways of avoiding or protecting ourselves from further pain. All sorts of people may have hurt us in the past, sometimes knowingly, often unintentionally. A teacher may have undermined our self-confidence by implying we'd never be any good. A relative may have made us feel unhappy about our appearance by personal remarks about our features. But by far the largest part of all the damage will have been done by our parents, simply because they were the ones with the most opportunity and greatest power to affect us.

The sort of damage parents can cause can vary immensely from outright abuse, sexual or verbal, to the subtle effects of criticism, a lack of expressed love, or a conditional acceptance based on unrelenting high standards. Most of us find it very hard to own up to the damage our parents caused in us. It is almost as if we are wired up to excuse them, we want to believe they did not mean to hurt us and for most people that is true, their parents were doing their best. It's also disagreeable to think that our parents damaged us because it must mean that we are capable of damaging our own children. So what's to be gained by owning up to all this unintentional hurt? After all, there is no benefit in trying to change our parents now. What *is* possible, though, is that we are more likely to be able to change the way we behave, when we understand why we behave that way. For example, maybe we were babied or belittled and never fully made to believe that we were capable of anything or maybe we were relied on too much and now we struggle to let anyone else take responsibility. Owning up to the way we were hurt can often throw light on the way we behave now. Understanding how we were victims can help us change.

Becoming a parent ourselves can often be a time when we reflect on the way we ourselves were parented. We see our parents in a new light when we ourselves face the struggles of parenthood. We may feel more understanding for them or we may feel bitter towards them for the ways we perceive that they let us down. We may not think about our parents very much at all, but you can be sure that one way or another, the way you were parented will show itself sooner or later in the way you parent your children.

WHAT WAS MISSING FROM OUR CHILDHOOD?

So in what ways might our parents have damaged us? Many Christian psychologists and writers have thought long and hard about what are the basic longings of every human being. For the sake of simplicity I'm going to use the very helpful description of human longings developed by Larry Crabb.[2] His counselling model is based on the understanding that every human being is born with two basic personal longings. These longings are a valid and legitimate part of our nature, they are there because we are made in the image of God. Of course we all need food, shelter and warmth in order to survive, but in order to thrive we were made to have these other two longings met by living in dependency on the God who created us. The two most fundamental longings that we have are *a longing for security* and *a longing for significance*. To put it another way, we long for relationship and we long for impact. We long to be loved, to belong, to be unconditionally accepted, and we long to feel competent, valued, to have a sense of self-worth. From a very young age, we seek to fulfil these longings through all our relationships and activities, but these longings can only be fully met by being in relationship with God.

The way in which these longings were not fulfilled was the first way in which we were disappointed and damaged. This was not, entirely, our parents' fault; they could not fully meet them because they were not perfect parents any more than we are. Ever since childhood we have found ways of coping with life and managing our disappointment, ways that for many of us did not include depending on God. God's desire is for us to bring these longings to him so that he can meet them, to abandon our own methods for securing love and making an impact and to learn to depend on the resources of his unconditional love and rely on the value he bestows on us by making us his children.

That early damage and disappointment shows itself in the way you behave. It may be that you are now a perfectionist, never satisfied with what you do or with your kids' efforts, because you grew up believing that what you did was never good enough. Or you may find it hard to express emotions such as affection. Perhaps you are emotionally withdrawn because you were hurt by someone you trusted. Maybe you are crippled with fear and anxiety because you were rarely given any responsibility.

Do you see now how understanding that we are victims of sin begins to answer the question 'why are we agents of sin'? Maybe those sarcastic remarks are because you feel uncomfortable about sincere appreciation because you've never been sincerely appreciated? 'Surveying the damage' is a necessary process that must take place before any repair work can begin. The point of this process is not to apportion blame: it is not your fault, nor was it entirely your parents' fault. There is no value in going back to them and blaming them. This would just be another way of abdicating responsibility for your behaviour. God asks us to treat our parents with the same love, respect and forgiveness that reflects the way God treats us. It is true that we are victims, but it is still true that we are now responsible for the ways we choose to behave. We are called to account for sinful actions even though these actions are linked to the way we have been damaged.

'But I can't help the way I am,' you say. 'If it's true that it's my upbringing that's at fault, how can you make me responsible for my actions?' Or to put it in more concrete terms, 'How can you hold me responsible for my constant anxiety? I was so often criticised as a child I've grown up never being sure about any decision I make.'

If there were no other way out of your situation I admit that to make you responsible would seem unfair. All that can be done is to make the best of it. However there is a way forward from this dilemma; if having imperfect parents ourselves is one of the main reasons we are now such imperfect parents, then the only thing to do is to go back and start all over again with a perfect parent.

Apart from the fact that this would be a physical impossibility there aren't any perfect parents around. Or are there? Nicodemus, a man who came to Jesus looking for answers, asked this very question. 'How can a man be born when he is old . . . Surely he cannot enter a second time into his mother's womb to be born?' (John 3:4) What prompted Nicodemus to wonder about this? It was because Jesus had just told him that he must be 'born again'.

Over the years a lot of associated notions have cluttered the phrase 'born again'. These have clouded our understanding and deadened the impact of the original remark. Jesus' intention was not for us to go back over the same life and 'get it right this time' but to start life over again with a new family and a new parent: the one perfect parent, God himself. In the next chapter we are going to discover how hurts from the past can be healed and our needs for today met in full when we find God to be our 'perfect parent'.

The Answer is . . .

Dear God,
I have a problem,
It's me.
Dear Child,
I have an answer,
It's Me.

Susan Lenzkes[3]

CHAPTER FOUR

Finding the Perfect Parent in God

It used to be the case that you could choose your friends but as far as your family was concerned, you were stuck with what you'd got. Nowadays, for parents at least, this is no longer strictly true. Genetically, it is now possible for parents to have some influence over the type of child they conceive. It seems a little unfair, to me, that this influence is only one way. No child has ever been given the opportunity to say what type of parents it would like!

This raises an interesting question. If you could have chosen your parents, what qualities would you have looked for? Talent? Good looks? Intelligence? Or perhaps someone with money and power? In fact, none of these factors give any guarantee of that person making a good parent (a great comfort for those of us low in the good looks and intelligence stakes!). As we have already seen, there are only two essential longings any child has and any parent can go some way towards meeting these longings regardless of their financial or social status. Any parent can give their child 1) the gift of being loved and unconditionally accepted and 2) the gift of meaning and personal value. These gifts meet, in part, the child's longings for security and significance which we talked about in the last chapter. However, only God can be a perfect parent so it follows that God is the only one who is able to impart these gifts in their full measure. He is the only one who is able to make us feel deeply loved and accepted. God is the only one who can impart meaning to us, meaning and value that is based on who we are, not on how well we do our jobs or on how well-liked we are. If we are able to choose to become his child, in other words to choose our own perfect parent by being 'born again', as Jesus said to Nicodemus, what sort of parent would we be getting? What is God like? Many people hold different views of him. We'll start by looking at two common misconceptions.

GOD IS INDIFFERENT

The first misconception is this: God is indifferent. He doesn't really care about me, my concerns are of no importance to him. The details of my life are far too petty for him to be bothered with. For many people, even Christians, this attitude has become so much a part of the way they think that it deeply influences their whole approach to life. If people we know and see can be indifferent and uncaring, how can God, who seems so distant and unknowable, really care for us?

Recalling an incident from my childhood helped me to understand this question. It took place on a beach somewhere in the south of England when I was about ten years old. I was staying at a campsite with my Mum and Dad. On one particularly blowy morning Dad invited me to join him for a walk before lunch. He wanted to walk from the campsite out to one headland, then along the beach to the next headland and then back to the campsite. I fell in with this plan but when we reached the first headland I took one look at the mile-long beach curving away into the distance and opted for a leisurely retreat back to the campsite. Dad, who was never one to retrace his steps, decided to go on alone and we parted amicably. It took me a few moments after his departure to realise that I couldn't find the path back to the campsite. It had come on to the headland between some bushes but suddenly all the bushes look the same. I stood dithering for a while, aware that all the time my father was forging his way across the beach and further away from me. Eventually I reasoned that if I couldn't find my way back I'd better chase after Dad, who I could still see a few hundred yards ahead of me across the beach. Starting to run across the soft dry sand, I realised that catching up with him was not going to be all that easy, especially as he kept being hidden from view amongst the holiday makers. When I felt I was closing on him a little, I tried calling him but the words were just blown over my shoulder by the sea breeze. By then I was feeling afraid, annoyed and hurt all at the same time.

'If only he'd slow down, if only he'd glance round, just the once, if only he could hear me.'

I knew it was unreasonable but I felt that somehow he ought to just *know* that I was struggling along behind, needing him. He seemed so unaware, indifferent even. At last as we reach the next headland he turned and caught sight of me. Flooded with relief I raced forward and flung myself into his arms.

This memory remained in the back of my mind for many years, rarely recalled and without any meaning or significance until a time in my life when I was feeling very low and discouraged. There were lots of factors, but primarily the sheer hard work of caring for small children had left me feeling exhausted and depressed. One day, in a casual conversation, a friend remarked, 'Yes, but you *know* your Heavenly Father cares for you, don't you?'

'Does he?' I thought to myself. 'Does he really know how tired I am? Has he noticed all the effort I'm making? Does he see my fear and anxiety?'

'Well, Father,' I asked him, 'do you care?'

In the silence that followed my outburst, it was this

memory that flooded vividly through my mind. Watching it replay, I sensed God saying, 'That's how you are feeling about me, you are angry with me, disappointed in me, you feel hurt.' There was no sense of condemnation in this statement, no sense that I 'ought' not to feel this way. Nor were there any loud protests that my perception of him was wrong. It was as if God was simply allowing me to own up to how I was feeling. As I did just that, I must admit to feeling slightly disappointed that my admission didn't cause him to rush in and overwhelm me with a sense of his love and his presence. For several weeks nothing changed and I wondered why God had brought that memory to mind since it only seemed to make me feel worse. What I longed for was to have all the bad feelings taken away and replaced by a set of good feelings. But a set of feelings would not have been a safe basis for trust.

It took me some time to see that God wanted me to place my trust in the facts, not in my feelings. The fact was that God did love me, in spite of how I felt. He was not indifferent to my pain. He had shown me how much he loved me once and for all, when he gave his Son to die for me, and no further proof was needed. He was, in fact, graciously and regularly restating his love for me through the loving care I received from other Christians. The trouble was I was often too deafened by my depression to hear him.

GOD IS OUT TO GET ME

Some people think that the only reason God is interested in them is to see if they are behaving themselves. They see God as someone who disapproves of them, someone who is always out to tell them off, catch them out, someone who is keeping a list of their failings. For them God is someone they have to please by trying hard, rather like a strict but weary teacher who writes 'Tries hard but could do better' at the end of their every report. Anyone labouring under this misconception can feel crushed by her own failure to stick to regular disciplines such as having a daily quiet time, disciplines that are very hard to maintain when you have a house full of young children. Angela Ashwin, in her excellent book *Patterns not Padlocks*,[1] says, about this problem of false guilt:

> we need to be freed from the distorted idea that God is a stern, Victorian headmaster who will make us grovel for not sticking to a fixed time of daily prayer. God is with us in our life as parents, and not 'out there', pointing an accusing finger from a distance.

God gave us our children, he knows how demanding they are. He knows how tired we are. He is not a hard and uncaring task-master, or else why would he have said, 'Come to me, all you who are weary and burdened, and I will give you rest. Take my yoke upon you and learn from me, for I am gentle and humble in heart, and you will find rest for your souls' (Matthew 11:28–29).

SO WHAT *DO* WE KNOW ABOUT GOD?

The Bible provides us with many promises and facts that reveal God's character, like the one above. There are many lovely images that show us what he is like. Few reveal more about his tenderness and care for us than the image of God as a shepherd. This is the way Isaiah describes God's relationship with his people: 'He tends his flock like a shepherd: He gathers the lambs in his arms and carries them close to his heart; *he gently leads those that have young*' (Isaiah 40:11, emphasis mine).

Jesus echoed this image when he declared himself to be

the 'good shepherd', who knows and lays down his life for the sheep (John 10:14–15). We are reassured in Hebrews 4:15 that we have a high priest, although not one who is unable to sympathise but one who was tempted in every way just as we are.

If these can be said to be the facts about God; that he is for us, he is with us, he is on our side and he cares for us, how can we square these facts with the painful realities of our daily lives such as heart-ache, disappointment and difficult relationships? We find it hard to hold a view of a loving and caring God in balance with the harsh realities of life. Picture this dilemma as a see-saw: at one end we have a bundle of beliefs labelled 'God is good – Life goes well' and at the other end a bundle of beliefs labelled 'God is indifferent – Life hurts'. We may want to believe in a God who is a loving shepherd but we cannot balance that see-saw; our view of the world alters our view of God as we go up and down with life's events.

In fact God does not change as the circumstances of our lives change. His loving and trustworthy character is a fixed point, a stable base. Life is more like a ride on a swing than a go on a see-saw. Just like a child on a swing, our life swings up into the sunshine of good times and down into the shadows of bad experiences and our emotions, quite naturally, follow our circumstances. Our view of God, however, need not depend on whether the swing is up or down because God is the fixed bar, he is the stable frame to which the swing is attached. Our security on that swing does not depend on its position or speed but on the stable nature of the supporting frame. So in life, our security need not rest in the nature of the circumstances around us but in the unchangeable reliability of God.

So how do we hang on to a right view of God being our loving and caring parent when life is giving us a hard time? God does not expect us to deny our painful emotions. It is unrealistic for us to expect our head knowledge about God to inform our emotions that 'all is well' when it doesn't look that way. Clinging on to a right view about God may not alter our emotions but it can alter and inform our behaviour.

Sometimes the only way to hold on to the truth about God is by our fingertips, by faith 'as small as a mustard seed' (Matthew 17:20). It is often only with a whisper of faith that we exercise our will to declare our trust in God's faithful and loving nature. This kind of faith operates when there is no external evidence for our ears to hear, our eyes to see or our feelings to latch on to. This kind of faith honours God (Hebrews 11:1, 6).

At one of my lowest moments, when I had only enough faith to believe God would hear me and not enough faith to believe that he cared for me, I shouted at God, 'How can you know how I feel? You were never a mother.'

One of the great things about God is that he never breaks bruised reeds (Isaiah 42:3) and I was feeling very bruised when I blurted out that rebuke. He didn't go off in a huff, he didn't withdraw his care for me; when we shout arrogantly about our pain he is silently compassionate, not aggressively defensive.

Only recently did I discover some verses where God does describe himself as mother:

Can a mother forget the baby at her breast and have no compassion on the child she has borne? Though she may forget, I will not forget you! See, I have engraved you on the palms of my hands (Isaiah 49:15–16).

God is saying what every mother knows to be true – that, with all the feeding and caring, it is extremely unlikely that a mother would forget her child. He then adds that if human mothers cannot be indifferent towards their children, then how much more unlikely it is that God would forget us. Why is it unlikely? Because 'I have engraved you on the palms of my hands'. Whatever else that phrase meant at the time, it surely also points forward to the cross of Christ, when God did literally allow our sins to drive the nails through the hands of Jesus, his Son. Jesus' death on the cross is total proof that God loves me. He does not owe me any further explanations or proof.

Learning to live the life of faith as a parent is about learning who God is, learning that he has demonstrated his total love for me and learning to depend on that demonstration as sufficient evidence that God is on my side.

WHAT DIFFERENCE DOES THIS MAKE TO ME?

If I tell you that God does love you and is not indifferent to you and yet at the same time tell you that this will not automatically make you feel better, you may be forgiven for thinking, 'Why bother with God?' As the one who created us, God is the only one who can fully meet our human longings to be unconditionally loved and to have value and purpose. Having these longings fully met by a relationship with him may not automatically alter our feelings about life but it does have the power to alter our response to life's events. The more fully we recognise that our own longings are met, the less self-preoccupied we will be and the better we will be able to function as a parent – or in any other relationship, for that matter.

Let's now have a closer at how a relationship with God can meet these two basic longings.

OUR LONGING FOR SECURITY

God's love for us is unconditional; that means it is not based on our performance. Perhaps many of us started out on the Christian life believing Ephesians 2:8–9: 'For it is by grace you have been saved through faith – and *this is not from yourselves*, it is the gift of God – not by works, so that no one can boast' (emphasis mine). But then having believed that at the start, we've continued on the Christian life believing that God will only continue to love us if we reach some level of acceptable performance as a Christian. If we feel we don't measure up we go around with the notion that God is only tolerating us. The fact is there never has been nor will there ever be any way of earning God's favour but he has given it to us anyway, 'For God demonstrates his own love for us in this: While we were yet sinners, Christ died for us' (Romans 5:8). There are many facts about God's love packed into just a few verses in chapter 8 of Romans: his love is not begrudging or half-hearted, he allows us to call him 'Abba' or Daddy, he's made us co-heirs with his own son. He's promised that nothing can ever separate us from his love. There are many other passages in which God demonstrates that he loves us in a way that can allow us to feel totally secure, not merely tolerated.

OUR LONGING FOR SIGNIFICANCE

How significant am I to God? This is the same as saying what value do I have to God? What am I worth? Each of us needs to know that we matter, that we count. 1 Peter 1:18–19 tells us that we were not redeemed (paid for) by perishable things, like gold or silver but the price God paid for us was 'the precious blood of Christ'. God could not possibly have paid a higher price for me. That means I am of infinite worth.

It is often our sense of worth that is most battered by parenthood. If we have been busy with a career or have had a fulfilling ministry at our church then dropping out of these things into the full-time care of small children can almost destroy our sense of self-worth. Nobody sees how hard you work as a parent, there is no pay, no promotion, no bonus payments, few 'thank you's and no outward signs of being valued. Society at large underrates you and the very people you are serving (your children) are the least likely to express their appreciation and even if they do, no one else notices that you've played the 'Postman Pat' game all morning! In the early days of motherhood, when I'd succeeded in getting myself dressed, the baby dressed and both of us out to the shops, I longed for someone to come along and say, 'Well done, you're doing really well'. No one ever did. For all these reasons it is essential for parents to have their self-worth firmly rooted in God – when no one else values us we have to know how much God values us. It helps me enormously to know that God chose me (John 15:16). I have to believe he knew what he was doing when he did so. It also helps me to know that he holds my life and my future in his hands (Jeremiah 29:11). Whenever I don't feel up to the tasks he has entrusted to me (be it child care or work or whatever else), it helps me to know that through his Holy Spirit he has provided all that I need in terms of gifts and strength (2 Peter 1:3, Philippians 4:13, 2 Corinthians 9:8). I am of such value to him that he knows how many hairs are on my head (Matthew 10:30) and he has called me by name (Isaiah 43:1).

Learning to base our lives on these facts is a slow process. The deeper they sink into our thinking the more they will influence how we respond to life's events. The sticking point for many Christians in this process is that they hang around waiting until they 'feel' that these facts are true, instead of going ahead anyway and behaving and responding to people and situations in the way that they would if they knew the facts were true. Only when we respond with obedience and faith do we really start to know and believe the truth about God. No amount of learning verses or praying will fix the truth in our hearts as much as one step of faith. When we respond in obedience God's Holy Spirit writes the truth about God on our hearts.

Think of it this way: most of us have no problem believing that planes fly. Perhaps because we understand jet propulsion engines, or maybe because we can explain the laws of aerodynamics. Or we may simply believe they fly because we see them fly. The best demonstration of our belief is when we actually get into a plane and fly somewhere. The evidence of our feelings whilst in flight (confident or terrified) does not alter the plane's efficiency in flight. In just such a way, God is solidly and reliably God regardless of how we feel about him. When we respond in obedience and faith to the truth about God, our heart begins to receive the message our head has believed. Here is a list of some of the changes that might result in our behaviour if we base our lives on a true understanding about God. By acknowledging God to be our perfect parent and allowing him to meet our needs for security and significance then our response to difficult situations may be changed. For example:

◆ I need not feel envious of other people's success: business, financial or family, because I know my need to feel significant is met fully in God, I do not need to supplement it in terms of status or prestige.
◆ My world need not fall apart when I am criticised or slighted by someone I love, if I know that I am securely loved by God.
◆ I will not need to compete with or try to impress my fellow Christians, if I know I have my own unique part to play in God's family, and in my own.
◆ I can find the strength to respond lovingly when my own parents fail to understand me or seem not to accept me, if I know it is my Heavenly Father's view of me that counts.
◆ If I know I am significant to God right now, as I am,

I will be freed from unnecessary anxiety about not appearing to be doing anything 'spiritual'.

◆ I can respond in an unconditionally loving way to my children's success or failure once I am freed from proving my own worth and competence through the success of my children.

◆ I need not be swept away by someone who judges me without taking the time to understand me, because I know God is on my side and understands me.

◆ I can be free to serve others without needing to be noticed, without drawing attention to myself, when I know God sees and values all I do in secret.

◆ I can be free to be who I am and not try to bend myself into the type of person other people feel I should be, when I know that God made me and loves me. I need not crave the approval of others. God's approval is sufficient.

Do you notice how very practical are all the outcomes of taking all these spiritual truths to heart? If we base our life on the truth of how God sees us then our behaviour should be affected and when you start looking closely at many of our behaviour patterns it is amazing how many of them are related to our craving for significance and security.

If all these situations sound rather more like we should be, rather than how we actually are, if they sound too unlikely and far off for us to aim at, then it may help to remember that many a biblical hero achieved far more than they expected when they stepped out in faith with their knees knocking and their heart pounding: Moses was timid, Gideon was uncertain, Jonah was miserable, Elijah was depressed and Job was angry!

Learning to live a life of faith as a parent is about learning to base our lives on the truth of who God is. This is often a shaky and scary process. Sometimes it will feel that we are only holding on to that truth by our fingertips. As we grow in our dependence on God the truth about him will steadily become a solid base for our lives. In the last chapter of this book we will come back to ways of developing this growing dependence on God. So far we've talked about who he is, how he sees us and finally about the difference it can make to see ourselves as God sees us. The trouble is most of us are far more preoccupied with the way others see us.

CHAPTER FIVE

Be Yourself

How is it that a pile of cardboard boxes and used loo rolls, stuck together with sellotape, can reduce me to a blubbering heap of self-condemnation? I was staying at a friend's house and while I was doing some ironing in her utility room I saw it: a suspicious pile of boxes lurking in the corner with some papier maché shapes. Doubtless these were being hoarded as part of some ongoing craft project and would be used with the paint, glue and scrap material neatly saved up on the shelves above. I felt I was in the private stock-room of a creative genius and went weak at the knees with a sense of my own inadequacy.

Now, speaking personally, I'm not into boxes; saving them, painting them, and making 'Mega Subtronic Space Stations' out of them. I tell myself we haven't the space to keep them but the truth is I just do not enjoy sticking; glue makes me very harassed and just the thought of papier maché brings me out in a cold sweat. Crayons and playdough are about my limit. I have a friend who can cut out clever little moving spiders with one hand while making home baked cookies with the other. Needless to say my children love going to play at her house. They come home with fistfuls of hand-made gingerbread men and collages and my friend says, 'They were so good, I've even tiled half the kitchen.'

A few years ago someone of such competence would

have had me retreating, feeling like a mega wimp Mum. Now, I just stand in awe, love her to bits and send my kids round to play as frequently as possible! After years of self-condemnation, I hope I've learned to relax and be the sort of Mum I am.

Mind you, it isn't easy reaching that point of self-acceptance. The starting point, as we saw in the last chapter, is understanding how God sees us and knowing deep down how much he loves, accepts and values us. If we really believe that he made us the sort of person we are, it ought to matter less and less what other people think of us. I say 'ought to' because we are all human and unfortunately most of us spend far too much time judging ourselves against other people's standards instead of God's. It's our feeling of insecurity that leads us to rate or measure ourselves up against other people; we want to know how well we're doing and comparing ourselves with others seems to be the easiest way of finding out.

WHO SETS THE STANDARDS

Most of us believe in theory that God's view of us is all that counts but in practice we behave as if adherence to some code of acceptable normality was all that mattered. Unfortunately in our search to discover what is normal and acceptable, we rate and pigeon-hole other parents on to a sliding scale, starting with those we admire and imitate and going down to those we consider to be inadequate. We hope that we will come comfortably somewhere in the middle, near the 'normal and acceptable' mark. In case you think you've never played this game let me spell out for you a typical sliding scale. Your personal version of this scale may well be different but I'd be surprised if you weren't familiar with at least some of the personalities that feature on this one.

First let me introduce you to Jenny and Mike. Jenny is an 'earth mother'; her babies wear terry nappies, the children sip herbal drinks and they all wear unbleached cotton t-shirts printed with 'green' slogans. Next to them on this scale is Mary. Now Mary is an 'Oxo' Mum, the home-maker; home-made biscuits, heart-warming stews and hand-knitted jumpers, you name it and Mary can bake it, knit it or create it in cross-stitch. Next to her there's Paula, the 'career' Mum. Her children wear bright designer clothes (she can afford them!) and go to a private nursery. Paula's life is neatly organised into her Filofax.

So far you may be smiling, because written down like this these glib pictures of people sound ridiculous. But are they familiar? If they are, if you have ever characterised people in this way, did you realise you were judging them when you did so? Let's go to the other end of the scale and maybe the danger in this game will become obvious. Let's meet Helen and Peter. When they read that God said 'Be fruitful and increase in number' they took it personally. They have four children under five years of age, permanent bags under their eyes and a chaotic household. Why on earth didn't they use contraceptives more effectively? Then there's Mark, the 'lone ranger' parent; his two sons carry toy guns into church each week and seem intent on a Sunday school massacre. Finally there is Caroline, always at the back of church and at the edge of events; her kids are a bit grubby, they have runny noses all year round and are never more than one foot away from her.

By now I hope you can see the harm in labelling people like this. Putting people on a pedestal is one extreme of the way we respond to others, putting people down is the other. We make ourselves feel better by ridiculing other parents, sometimes because we secretly admire them or because their ability makes us feel threatened. On the other hand we could let the way others run their lives become an impossible model which we try to imitate without success. Either way, and especially at the lower end of the scale, a distance is created that prevents us from understanding that all parents, no matter how we rate them, are human too and have their own struggles and fears.

How do we know, for example, that the working mother we so admire doesn't worry endlessly over whether she has made the right choice for the family? She may even envy me my endless, unstructured days spent entertaining the children. Maybe Helen and Peter prayerfully planned their large family but are made to feel defensive and self-conscious by my unconscious implication that a neat well-spaced two-some is somehow better. Maybe Caroline, a lone parent struggling on a tight budget, is doing far better than we could do in similar circumstances.

Why do we consider some parents less effective, without ever stopping to get alongside them and understand their lives from their point of view? Jesus didn't judge people by appearance or by other people's view of them. Things couldn't really have looked worse for the woman caught in adultery and as for Zacchaeus, he was utterly despised by the crowd, but neither of these people received condemnation from Jesus. He took time to understand the whole story and he took time to affirm these two as individuals who mattered to God.

Instead of affirming people, we actually harm them by making quick judgements about them. We harm them because we fawn on them or because we despise them instead of just accepting and respecting them. It's important to note here that respect and acceptance does not mean we should condone or turn a blind eye to a clearly sinful pattern of behaviour. Jesus told the woman to 'go and sin no more', he did not condone adultery. Zacchaeus' response to Jesus was to pay back over and above what he had cheated. Clearly we cannot condone or accept sinful behaviour but we must respect and affirm sinful people as being made in God's image and as having infinite worth to him. We need to learn how to relate to one another in love as children of the same Heavenly Father, not as superior or inferior rivals.

Apart from harming other people by making quick judgements we also harm ourselves. It may not seem obvious at first how judging someone else could harm us but it does because we rack up our self-esteem by looking at others who seem worse than we are, or we tear down our self-esteem by looking at those who are doing better than we are. The basis for healthy self-esteem does not lie in how others see us or in how we rate ourselves, it lies in how God sees us. He made us. He gave us our talents, abilities and personalities. He chose us to be the parents of the children he chose to give us and he loves us. It takes us so long to learn this and sometimes even when we think we've learned it we 'wobble' in our self-view when someone more competent comes along.

I felt so condemned by that pile of cardboard boxes I mentioned earlier that we did, in fact, attempt a cereal packet creation of our own. It became a town planner's nightmare. I envisaged a whole village of little box houses with smart red roofs and roses round the doors. Yes, I know it was too ambitious. If my daughter wanted ten factories with one window and five doors each I should have left well alone. Instead of that we all got cross and fell out. I've now decided to leave model making until she is totally competent with glue, scissors and sellotape and then combine her with them in a safe but distant place (the garage?) and await the result.

Now I've confessed that I'm hopelessly inept at craft and creativity I expect that half of you reading this will feel a warm glow of self-satisfaction because you love it and the other half will feel a huge sense of relief that someone else will admit to being uninspired by egg-boxes. So, now you're all feeling good let me pass on the first lesson I learned en route to self-acceptance.

PLAY TO YOUR STRENGTHS

Before you think this sounds rather big-headed and unscriptural, it is in fact only a positive outcome of a rather negative-sounding command found in Romans 12:3: 'Do not think more highly of yourselves than you ought but rather think of yourselves with sober judgement in accordance with the measure of faith God has given you.'

The main point this verse makes is that we should not be proud or conceited about our talents and abilities because everything we have and are comes from God anyway. 'Sober judgement' is a phrase used to puncture any 'self-important' view we may have of ourselves and quite right too. But does 'sober judgement' mean we should feel miserable about ourselves? I don't think so. Rather it involves an honest assessment, deciding what we are good at and what we find easy. I like what the eighteenth-century commentator, Matthew Henry has to say about this verse:

As we must not on the one hand be proud of our talents, so on the other hand we must not say, 'I am nothing, therefore I will sit still and do nothing'; but, 'I am nothing in myself, and therefore will lay myself out to the utmost in the strength of the grace of Christ.'[1]

Many of us feel under pressure to be an all-singing, dancing, juggling, creative parent with a degree in the 'right' way to nurture children. We can cave in under this pressure. This verse reminds us that we do not have to be talented at everything, the talents we do have are from God anyway so let's not worry overly about the talents we were not given.

I'm not saying we shouldn't aim at being the best parent we can possibly be. We do have to take responsibility for those things that can damage our relationships. We cannot condone, in ourselves, sinful behaviour patterns such as a continual bad temper, a nagging, critical tone or even the subtle withdrawal of expressed love and approval to a child who is driving us barmy. All these things are matters for repentance and renewed commitment to behave in a godly and responsible way, a commitment we can only fulfil by depending on God's daily help and empowering.

As far as the sort of personality, talents, and interests we have, we need to learn to relax and be who we are instead of trying to be everything for our children. I am the sort of Mum who likes reading stories. I enjoy attempts at making music. I like talking and I don't mind board games (I come into my own on a rainy day). I also like rowdy games of 'roary lions' and outdoor running about games. I do not thrive on messy play, I find it just so . . . messy really. I have found ways of tolerating it. Our sandpit is at the very end of the garden; that way most of the sand is shaken off before the happy digger arrives at the back door. Painting is allowed only in fine weather and as close as possible to the outside tap. Cooking is okay as long as I see it as a quick boost to the blood sugar level and not a serious attempt to produce something edible. Once you know your inabilities you can sometimes find ways to work round them.

KNOW YOUR LIMITATIONS

Being able to play to your strengths is one thing. The other side of this process of self-assessment is to know your limitations by being aware of your inabilities. My incompetence with glue, scissors and egg-boxes is something I am aware of but choose to overlook whenever it's convenient. It's only when I see someone else succeeding in my area of weakness that the guilt-laden 'blubbering heap' syndrome comes into play. In such a situation a second verse is very helpful if taken into our hearts and minds: 'Each one should test his own actions. Then he (or she) can take pride in himself, without comparing himself to someone else' (Galatians 6:4).

In other words we are not to let other people's abilities or lack of them be the measure by which we judge our worth. Matthew Henry puts it well: 'The better we are acquainted with our own hearts and ways, the less liable shall we be to despise and the more disposed to be compassionate and help others.'[2]

We don't have to carry unnecessary, self-imposed guilt just because we're not gifted in the same way as others, just because we're not musical nor green-fingered, for example. God has designed us all differently and we each have a unique combination of gifts, abilities and preferences which we bring to our children. Now whenever I see a collage of pasta shapes I say loudly to myself, 'My children are not going to grow up warped and deprived just because I can rarely bring myself to messy creativity.' Maybe all you clever Mums and PPA members are tut-tutting with disapproval but at least I have learnt simply to enjoy your competence. I'll sign up for your playgroup and you can have my kids to play any time. What is the point of me attempting something that just makes us all hot and bothered? I cannot be you but I can be me to the best of my ability.

Whenever the clamour for paint, mess or glue gets too much in our house we go out. We go out a lot: the park, the library, a round trip on the bus if we're desperate. Now it makes a lot of sense to know your limitations whenever you are out and about with the kids. My kids are limited by distance and appetite. Unlike my sister's children, who will walk for miles and have a total disregard for meal times, mine will only go five hundred yards unaided and suffer complete limb failure if made to walk past lunchtime. I learnt this lesson the hard way. We had gone to a country park with a friend for the afternoon and she suggested that walking round the lake would be a pleasant way to spend the afternoon. I'd never been to this particular park before.

'How far is it?' I asked suspiciously, aware that through the foliage I couldn't actually see the end of the lake.

'Oh, not far, we've walked it loads of times.'

Inspired by her spirit of adventure I threw caution to the wind and we set off, my voice full of false enthusiasm. 'We're going to walk all the way round, won't it be fun?'

At the fore-mentioned five hundred yard mark my kids began requesting to be carried. This soon gave way to demands for juice or ice-cream. Needless to say we had no liquid refreshment with us and there were no ice-cream vans in sight. Trying not to be rude I suggested a U-turn might be more dignified.

'We've gone almost half way. It'll be just as quick to carry on,' she replied. Instead of admitting then that my children simply wouldn't walk round the lake I felt they 'ought to'. Her kids were clearly capable of it. Caving in under the pressure of comparison, I pressed on. I wish I'd known then that my friend had a very elastic sense of distance. One whole hour's walking/carrying later I found myself praying for a helicopter air lift back to the car park. When I felt I could go no further my prayers were answered, although not in such a dramatic way. Round the next bend there was a very welcome if rather bizarre sight: an abandoned shopping trolley. If you think heavily laden trolleys are difficult to push down shopping aisles you want to try taking a trolley full of whining kids on a woodland walk. I don't recommend it. You get some pretty funny looks too. My arms and back were aching but somehow we made it back to the car park and I vowed that never again would I be tempted to cross the boundaries of our known limitations.

Playing to my strengths and knowing my limitations were both lessons in self-acceptance that were summed up for me by a poster I once saw. It said, 'Be yourself, who else is better qualified?' I recommend this phrase to you, to be repeated to yourself every time someone else's capabilities tempt you to over-reach your own. In a safe environment do test out your limitations. I'm not giving you an excuse to simply say, 'I'm no good at that, and I never will be.' There is often room for improvement and mastering new skills, but when you do feel out of your depth don't berate yourself unnecessarily.

SO FAR SO GOOD

I hope that from all that we've covered in these first five chapters, you will be happy to be honest with yourself. If you didn't already know it, you are an imperfect parent. Join the club! You're in good company, we are all imperfect. I hope too that you've seen a new view of your security in God, a security that is not related to how well you feel you are doing as a parent. Finally in this chapter we've looked at a new way of relating to other parents, being able to accept them as they are and ourselves as we are.

With all these new outlooks on life, God 'and the universe', surely family life can now go on happily ever after? All we have to do is be honest with ourselves and keep our eyes on God, not on other people, and all will be well. Right? Well, yes, in theory that is right. The trouble is life is not lived in theory, it is lived in practice and in practice we will be ordinary failing human beings for the rest of our lives. This means that there will be many times when we will feel overwhelming negative emotions towards our fellow human beings, especially the small and unruly ones in our family. How on a practical day-to-day level do we handle such negative feelings in the light of the theory we've understood?

The second half of this book aims to answer that question by grounding the theory in the practicality of family life.

THE PRACTICE

CHAPTER SIX

Handling Those
'Hard-to-handle' Feelings

Being a parent could possibly be described as a journey from optimism to pessimism. It has been said that deciding to have a baby is an act of supreme optimism, an expression of hope and confidence in the future. It is likely that when you were a new parent you had all sorts of ideals and impossible expectations such as 'He'll never eat sweets' or 'We'll always understand each other'. Probably the sharply defined edges of those expectations were slowly sandpapered down by the 'fray' of family life and reshaped into something more realistic like 'Let's get through today cheerfully'. Sooner or later you may have realised that you are not the optimist and idealist you once were. Maybe it was when your 'perfect' baby decided that sleeping through the night wasn't such fun after all, or maybe it was when your two-year-old decided that she ruled the world, or perhaps it was when you realised that your son could argue better than you could, or maybe it was when your daughter reached puberty and all those hormonal surges changed your little girl into a moody, unresponsive and spotty stranger. Whenever it was, at some point you will have been tempted further along this journey toward pessimism. Perhaps you paused briefly at cynicism: 'What ever I do, it will always be the wrong thing to have done', before arriving finally at pessimism: 'Anything that can go wrong, will go wrong, so what's the use of hoping it'll all turn out well.'

The most contented parents I know are not necessarily the ones with the 'well-turned' out kids, but they are the ones who have learned the happy knack of stopping this journey at realism and refusing to be drawn into an embittered, pessimistic outlook. They accept things the way they are, but they always make the best of it. Whilst they are not short-sighted about their own or their kids' shortcomings they think the best of them and maintain a positive outlook.

How can we handle the down-side of parenting in a realistic and yet cheerful way? You may feel very disappointed that your expectations of parenthood have not always been met. Perhaps you never realised how restricting and awkward young children can be. Perhaps, like me, you have been unpleasantly surprised by just how annoyed, impatient or anxious your children can make you. I remember talking to an older friend at the end of a particularly bad day. His children were teenagers.

'Tell me about it,' he said, after I'd listed all the day's frustrations. 'The people I get the most angry with are the people who mean the most to me!'

Somehow I was really comforted by such an admission from this very mild-tempered father. There was no doubting that my friend loved his kids and I know that deep down I also love my children but I also know just how he feels. The fact is that no matter how overwhelmed you feel with love towards your 'cherub babe' on his arrival, he will sooner or later make you so angry or upset that the feeling of love will be too deep down to be of any practical use to you. This is entirely normal and a common experience of every parent.

It may be normal but it is still disappointing – especially if the negative feelings are so frequent that they leave us feeling overwhelmed, stressed out and fed up with family life. What's wrong with me? Why am I not enjoying this? Why can't I feel more relaxed with my kids? Why is there so much aggravation and hassle? I do love my kids, why doesn't that seem to make any difference? Why does every day feel like a battlefield?

Strong emotions such as these can leave parent-child relationships strained at best. At worst a coldness and hostility can creep in on both sides, making it ever harder for loving relationships to develop. What can you do when this happens? What can you do if you find yourself without either the inclination or the power to change the situation?

UNCONDITIONAL LOVE

The answer to all our difficult human relationships has to lie in our relationship to God. The connection may not seem obvious at first. In chapter three we concentrated on how God relates to us. Here's a brief reminder:

- He relates to us with unconditional love: 'But God demonstrates his own love for us in this: while we were still sinners, Christ died for us' (Romans 5:8).
- With complete forgiveness: 'If we confess our sins, he is faithful and just and will forgive us our sins and purify us from all unrighteousness' (1 John 1:9).
- His love gives us personal meaning and value: 'How great is the love the Father has lavished on us, that we should be called children of God! And that is what we are!' (1 John 3:1).
- He created me, knows me intimately and calls me by my name (Psalm 139, Isaiah 43:1).
- He chose me and is committed to me, he will not give up on me (John 15:16, Matthew 28:20).

• He has promised to provide all I need (2 Peter 1:3).

It is immensely reassuring to focus on the way God relates to us. It is immensely challenging when we realise that he requires that we relate to others in the same way. Now do you see the link between God's relationship with us and our relationships with the sometimes difficult and unruly members of our family? Is God's requirement fair? After all he's God, how can we as mere human beings love other people (especially the difficult ones) in the same way that God loves us? Is it really God's intention that we should be able to relate to people with the same unconditional love that he has for us? The Bible tells us that he does intend just that: 'As the Father has loved me, so I have loved you . . . love each other as I have loved you' (John 15: 9, 12).

God knows that on our own we are incapable of such love. That is why the answer to all our difficult relationships lies in our relationship to God. A relationship is always a growing thing and the more we grow in our relationship with God as our parent the more our own parenting style will reflect the qualities of God's love. The command, 'Be imitators of God . . . and live a life of love' (Ephesians 5:1), comes straight after a very practical section at the end of Ephesians 4 which details what unconditional love should look like, ending with the summary, 'Be kind and compassionate to one another, forgiving one another, just as in Christ God forgave you'. How can we do this? The answer is tucked away in the middle of the command in Ephesians 5:1. Let's read it in full: 'Be imitators of God, therefore, *as dearly loved children* and live a life of love, just as Christ loved us and gave himself up for us as a fragrant offering and sacrifice to God' (emphasis mine).

It is only as we enjoy a relationship with God as dearly loved children that we can begin to love others unconditionally in the other-centred and sacrificial way that Jesus loved us. When we know ourselves to be loved in this way we can aim towards being able to make the following statement: 'Being totally convinced that I am loved, and secure and confident of my own significance before God, I can behave towards others and towards events in a way that expresses my God-given wholeness.'

Faced with a difficult relationship or an awkward situation in your family, you may only be able to make such a statement through gritted teeth and you may only be able to respond lovingly through an exertion of your will in obedience rather than being motivated by any warm loving feelings. Don't let the absence of warm loving feelings put you off, they really don't matter very much.

If the thought of loving someone 'through gritted teeth' seems a shocking travesty of how you think God's love is meant to feel, let me remind you of John 14:15: 'If you love me, you will obey what I command.' Jesus says that love is demonstrated by obedience, not by warm feelings. He doesn't rule out the possibility of feeling good, but he doesn't require it as evidence of love; all he requires is obedience.

THE 'FEEL GOOD' FACTOR

Going right back to the 'flower power' era, there has been much emphasis on good feelings, 'Love is all you need', 'If it feels good do it'. An attitude persists in society that feelings are all that matter. A recent hit song had the lines,

> You know I love you and I always will,
> My mind's made up by the way that I feel.[1]

If the lover in the song has only his feelings to direct his decisions then heaven help the poor woman he loves when she wakes up sick, tired, ugly or 'unlovable' in any other way! We are all more influenced than we realise by these attitudes. Even the Christian community is not exempt from the influence of the 'feel good' factor.

All these influences lead us to think that we ought to feel good about being a parent, we ought to feel warmly affectionate towards our kids and if we don't always feel that way then there must be something wrong with us. As for bad feelings, society in general seems to hold the attitude that we have a right to vent these, however we like and whenever we like: it's called freedom of expression. The real danger of such attitudes is that they reinforce our deeply-held commitment to 'feeling good'. 'Doing the right thing' has lost its appeal, 'having a good feeling' seems a far more attractive option. If we are going to demonstrate unconditional love we will have to give up this commitment to feeling good because a demonstration of such love towards an objectionable, difficult or unresponsive child will not often cause us to 'feel' good. We must be careful not to fall into the trap of measuring the rightness of a course of action by the level of good feelings it gives us.

Imagine your child has generously invited half of his class to his birthday party. When your 'guests' arrive half of them are unknown to you and one little lad is rather grubby and dishevelled. He is somewhat short on social graces but worse than that, he has a permanent green stream from his nose. There is nothing about him that inspires warm loving feelings of tenderness and affection; rather the reverse, you find yourself grappling with feelings of revulsion and annoyance and wondering how you can avoid this situation next year. Will your children pick up his bad manners, his germs or both? In spite of these negative feelings you recognise that as your child has invited him, it would be best to make him feel welcomed and respected. How do you communicate that to the child? By your actions, you ensure he has a good seat at the table, has a turn of all the toys, that no one makes any remarks about him, you may even discreetly supply him with a tissue for his nose, but only to make him feel more comfortable and not because you can't bear to look at him. If this child leaves your party feeling loved and accepted it will be because of your actions. Your feelings will have had nothing to do with it. You exerted your will in line with your choice and behaved in a way that had his best interests at heart. The fact that you did not feel loving towards the child is neither here nor there.

We need to get rid of this notion that it is somehow wrong to behave in a way that goes against our feelings. As a parent a vast amount of our time is spent doing things that do not rate highly on the 'feel good' scale: changing nappies, spoon-feeding babies, getting up in the night, potty training, reading the same story endlessly, listening to the same terrible jokes and laughing faithfully every time, coaching a nervous child through swimming lessons, listening to sob stories when friends fall out. I could go on, but I think you get the picture: parenthood is a commitment to hard work. I could balance the above list with an equally long list of good times a parent is privileged to experience – there is plenty of 'job satisfaction' available – but if we are expecting to feel good most of the time, we are likely to be disappointed.

While we are learning how to love the other members of our family with this unconditional kind of love, it will often seem that to act lovingly will require us to go against our feelings. As I've already said, it is not wrong to act in a way that is inconsistent with our feelings, it is not somehow hypocritical or repressed. What we are choosing to do is to behave in a way that is consistent with our beliefs, i.e. if I know and believe that God loves me and values me I can find the strength to love another person even if that person does not respond well to me, even if they reject me or appear indifferent towards me.

WHAT FUELS UNCONDITIONAL LOVE?

If we are reliant on positive feed-back from the ones we are trying to love then we are not loving unconditionally and as parents we are sunk because children simply do not provide positive loving feed-back. They are not known for their fulsome expressions of appreciation for all their parents do for them. They do not say, 'Thanks, Mum, for caring enough about me even if it means I can't sleep over at Daniel's and watch horror films', or 'Thanks, Dad, for teaching me the value of things by making me save up for my own computer games'. We hope they will say things like this when they are adults, but as children they will never appreciate all the things you do for them. If you expect them to, your expectations are unrealistic and unhelpful. So if you can't keep loving because of their loving feed-back, how else can you keep on loving unconditionally? The answer is to know your value and your significance and to be sure you are getting these from the right source.

Being a parent is a lesson in servanthood, in giving and not counting the cost. Servanthood is not always a rewarding vocation and for many parents the quickest route back to having a sense of personal significance is through a return to a career or through any number of leisure pursuits that give a sense of fulfilment, a sense of 'doing something just for me'. It may be entirely appropriate to return to a career or to take up oil painting; there may be nothing wrong with doing either of these things. However, it is good to be aware that these activities provide us with a valid sense of significance, a sense of being in control, of making choices. Whether we decide to return to work or not, the important thing is not to rely on that job or activity to provide us with the sense of significance that only God can reliably provide. You could be made redundant through no fault of your own, or you might find that no one else appreciates your sense of 'art', or perhaps you've thrown yourself into some area of church life looking for fulfilment and some one new has arrived at church who is clearly more gifted than you in that area. What will happen to your sense of significance then? God does want us to live full, active lives exercising our talents and gifts but he will not allow us to replace him as the ultimate source of significance in our lives. There is no better time for learning this than when you are being the 'parent at home' in care of small children. Whether you are there through choice or are simply stuck with the situation, you will have discovered that there are few outside sources fuelling your sense of self-worth and significance; it becomes more important than ever to know who you are in God's eyes. It is just as important for your 'working parent' friends to know this, but it will not feel so important to them. If any of us end up relying on our jobs, our hobbies, our ministry or our kids for our sense of value then we are heading for trouble. Being a parent is giving without getting anything back. If we rely on our children's appreciation, response and affection to fuel our affection for our children then we will run dry pretty quick. It follows that if our children cannot fuel our desire to act lovingly then we had better know where we can find a reliable outside source of love and significance that can energise our attempts to love our families.

It might help for a minute if you can picture your home and family as being represented by the diagram of a house on the next page. This house is fitted with under-floor central heating. This keeps the place warm and cosy. The fuel for this warmth is love. With love underlying the home every relationship is warm and open and the home is a pleasant place to be. This is how we'd all like it to be in our family. The reality is that we do not always feel lovingly warm towards the other human beings in our family. Even if we do feel loving they may not be responsive, they may be aggressive or indifferent to our love. Eventually because we are fallen human beings there will be times when the bad feelings are so bad that it will feel like the love has run out and the home and relationships have grown cold and distant.

How can we prevent this from happening? There is only one thing to do and that is to plug our homes into

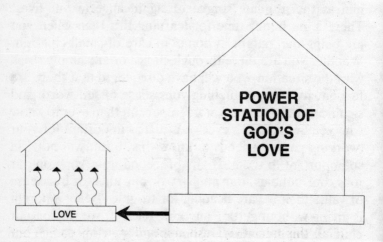

the mains, into a reliable outside supply of unending and unconditional love.

The way we do this is by basing our lives firmly on the fact that God loves us and values us, then we can choose to respond in a way that is consistent with this fact, not with our feelings. I'm not suggesting for a moment that this will be easy but it is the only way forward because love is a choice, an act of will, an action. Love is not necessarily a warm emotion.

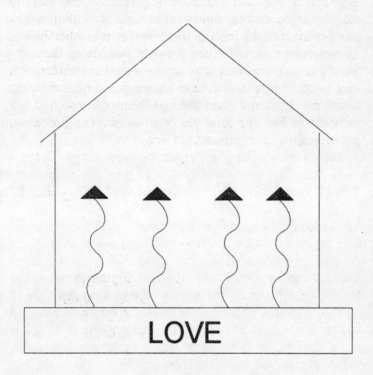

If all this talk about stiff upper-lipped obedience and loving through gritted teeth sounds rather barren and unappealing, I agree with you. It is. It is perfectly normal and legitimate for us to long to 'feel good' about our home-life, and it is reasonable to feel disappointed when we do not feel good about it. Plugging into God's supply of unconditional love may be the only way to respond lovingly in spite of these negative feelings, but will these negative feelings ever go away? Will you ever feel more patient, more relaxed, and less hassled? If you are committed to getting rid of the 'bad' feelings and only ever feeling the 'good' ones the answer to that question is probably 'No', because those bad feelings that you are suppressing will come out in some other way. None of us can live a life free from situations that give us bad feeling. If, however, you switch the focus of your attention away from your feelings, acknowledging them but deciding not to act according to them, then it may well be that the next time you check out your feelings you will find they will have come into line, and yes, you will start to feel more positive about parenthood.

WHAT DOES UNCONDITIONAL LOVE LOOK LIKE?

We have already seen from Ephesians 4 that unconditional love focuses on the needs of the other person. It is other-centred. It is also sacrificial; we are called to 'lay down our lives for our brothers' (1 John 3:16). Every command to love is backed up by the reminder that God loves us (1 John 4:11). This commitment to love is not to be pursued in holy isolation (which would be a lot easier!). Rather it is to be worked out in the nitty gritty of relationships. Look at Galatians 5 and you'll find commands to 'stop devouring and biting each other' in almost the same breath as 'serve one another in love' and 'The fruit of the Spirit is love'. Unconditional love is to be truthful (Ephesians 4:25) but truthfulness is not a licence to ride rough-shod over the needs of others. Instead our words should be limited by what is helpful to them (Ephesians 4:29); we are to be more concerned with what will build them up, rather than what will make us feel better. Sometimes unconditional love will be demonstrated by speaking up for our own needs and desires to be respected, at other times the best demonstration of unconditional love will be putting our needs and desires to one side.

Let me illustrate with a story. It's a story involving

my husband and as I have no God-given responsibility to discipline him or change him, you may think it is not a good illustration for learning to demonstrate unconditional love towards your children. However the principle is the same.

Every Saturday evening my husband cooks me a meal. It's a special time as it is the only meal in the week that we eat without the children and we try to make it a 'just for us' occasion. As we both love food, a good meal is a crucial factor for a successful evening. On one particular Saturday David had planned to do a curry. Now I like curries so long as they are not too hot. This curry was so hot it blew steam out your ears, and what's more, somewhere in the cooking process the good quality steak that he had used had been transformed into pieces of shoe leather. I came expectantly to the table when it was ready and we tucked in. After a few moments I suspected that my husband's mouth was lined with asbestos because he didn't seem to notice either the taste or the texture of the meal. More to the point, neither did he notice that I was playing with my food and left most of it. He cleared away cheerfully, without commenting on the fact that I was making myself a sandwich. I had recently been reading a book on marriage which had really challenged me to demonstrate unconditional love and I knew that in this instance love would not be best served by sounding off my feelings so I went to bed biting back all the sarcastic and hurtful remarks I felt like making about my husband's cooking. This didn't feel good, but it was better than giving vent to my disappointment in the destructive way that would have satisfied my anger. In the morning, before church I found myself still struggling with feelings of anger and hurt towards David. I was annoyed our evening had been spoilt and I was hurt he hadn't seemed to notice my disappointment. This may all sound rather over-dramatic, it was only a curry after all, but family life is made up of just such small incidents that spark big emotions. We all aspire to respond nobly over the big hurts and disappointments but in real life most of us fall flat on our faces when we are called to lovingly overlook the small hurts.

It was quite out of character for me not to have told David how I felt; usually he was informed 'in no uncertain terms'. As I talked over my feelings with God on the Sunday morning the 'conversation' ran something like this,

'Lord, if I don't tell him how I feel, he'll never notice of his own accord. What if he rides roughshod over my feelings again? Don't I have a right to express myself?'

'Not in a way that tears him down.'

'But Lord, what if he never notices how I feel, this is too hard, Lord.'

'This is unconditional love. This is the same love with which I loved you when I came and died, giving up all my rights to be understood, knowing that you might never believe in me and might always reject me.'

After quite a struggle I gave in and resolved to forgive David quietly in my own heart and let go of the anger. Knowing that God understood how I felt, I committed myself to loving David unconditionally, in my words and my actions. Only a few minutes after I'd finished praying, David came into the room, kissed me and said,

'You seem a bit upset this morning, I'm sure it's my fault but I can't think what I've done.'

After which remark I couldn't muster one single miserly feeling towards him, which was in itself rather annoying seeing as I'd nobly steeled myself to respond in line with my beliefs! The curry was not mentioned again until the middle of the following week, by which time all the 'heat' had gone out of the problem and I was able to express my feelings of disappointment in a way that did not make him feel threatened or undermined.

SO WHAT DO I DO WITH
MY NEGATIVE FEELINGS?

If we want to be loving in our actions, and for the sake of simplicity I am going to assume that most parents do, then we have to get round the problem of what to do with bad feelings. When I say that a feeling is bad or when I call it negative, I do not mean to label it as intrinsically sinful. Feelings are not 'bad' in the sense of being evil, they are merely 'bad' in the sense that they affect us negatively. Essentially there are only three things I can do with a 'bad' feeling: 1) I can blow up 2) I can bottle up or 3) I can own up.[2]

1) Choosing to blow up does not often feel like a conscious choice; it just tends to happen. None the less it is a choice, and we do not have to handle a negative feeling this way. It felt very hard, 'unnatural', 'repressed' even, to be biting back all those remarks about David's cookery skills and apparent indifference. My cultural conditioning tells me I have a right to be 'assertive', to make my feelings known, to 'vent'. The Bible doesn't say I have any such 'right'. Instead it says, 'Love bears all things, believes all things, hopes all things, endures all things' (1 Corinthians 13: 4–7), even hot curries! There is nothing wrong with a calm assertiveness that gives dignity and value to my views and opinions, but assertiveness should not be an excuse for an outpouring of destructive anger. If I am to truly love another person, whether that person is my husband or my child, I have to consider their needs and feelings before I do or say anything. I am not allowed to vent off in a way that would satisfy me but tear them down, because love builds up. My overriding concern has to be for the good of the other person. 'Speaking the truth in love' (Ephesians 4:15) is more often used as a pretext for sounding off about my feelings while trying to pin the blame on the other guy. It is a responsibility few should

aspire to because most of us would be wiser to keep quiet. It is appropriate for us to express our feelings but the limit on our expression must be the effect of our words and tone on the person to whom we are speaking. Their highest good is more important than my right to 'vent'.

2) The second choice I have is to 'bottle up'. This amounts to a refusal to acknowledge hurt and disappointment. This is unhelpful because anything that is pressed down and denied will find an outlet one way or another. It can also make us look ridiculous, like the man who jumped off the roof of a high building and was heard to be saying, as he passed every floor on his way towards a terminal encounter with the pavement, 'I'm okay so far, I'm okay so far'! God does not want us to have dishonesty as a defence mechanism against the unpleasant side of life.

3) So what's left? What can we choose to do? We can 'own up'. The most helpful person to own up to is God and this is what I got round to doing on the Sunday morning. It was only when I had expressed my disappointment to God that the gentle presence of the Holy Spirit could help me let go of my anger and, knowing he understood, I could then accept his help in committing myself to loving in his way.

Owing up is simply being honest with God about how we feel. Some Christians may feel uncomfortable about owning up to some very negative feelings, so it is worth saying at this point that a feeling is just a feeling, it is not a sin in itself. It's what we do with our feelings that is often sinful. We are allowed to express all our feelings to God, no matter how overwhelming or negative and sinful they might seem to be. Even a quick look in the Psalms will reveal just about every type of human emotion, ranging from despair, anger, jealousy, hopelessness, anxiety and fear to hope, joy, peace and faith. We somehow assume the latter emotions are intrinsically good and spiritual, and the former ones evil or harmful, when in fact all that these feelings are, are feelings. It is right and good that we own up to the full range before God. He will not condemn us, he understands us, he does not hold us to account for the feelings we experience, but he does hold us to account for the actions we take.

There are some feelings that are confusing, for example, is lust a feeling or a sin? Lust is a feeling of sexual desire that has been welcomed in, entertained by the mind and perverted. Jealousy is another such emotion; this is usually a feeling of low self-worth that has been entertained and perverted into a destructive desire towards another person. Feelings and sins do overlap, and 'owning up' and confession often do go hand in hand, but let's not automatically label every strong emotion as wrong. It's what we do with it that counts.

Most of our negative emotions will fit one way or another under one of three categories of feeling: anger, guilt and anxiety. The plan is not to find a way of avoiding these negative emotions, because they are an inevitable, unavoidable part of life. Rather we need to find ways in which we can respond lovingly in spite of our negative feelings.

To sum up then, there are in fact only two parts to your family's home: the foundation and the structure. The foundation is the unconditional love of God towards us, and the structure consists of the strategies we develop to demonstrate this love in our homes. In my experience most parenting books and courses lay heavy emphasis on the second part and not enough on the first. Any building erected without a foundation will quickly collapse. Not for nothing did Jesus describe himself as the rock on which to build. A growing, deepening trust in Jesus is the foundation that underpins, strengthens and holds the whole structure together. This is the only foundation worth laying; it is in essence the experience of God's love for you, flowing through to your kids. The only proper basis for all our relationships is learning to relate to others the way God relates to us.

The 'structure' of our home is simply made up of strategies: star-charts, family rules, positive reinforcement, corporal punishment, understanding your child's personality, all of these are just strategies. They are the walls, the door, the roof and windows of your home, if you like. There are books on every sort of strategy you'd like to choose. All of them work some of the time with some of the people; what works for me might not work for you. There is nothing wrong with strategies, but they have to be underpinned by something. So, before we look in more practical detail at the problems in our homes, I would like to make a plea that you don't let your desire for a new strategy, or a quick solution, allow you to overlook the hard work of laying the foundation. In other words don't get so preoccupied with the structure of your home, the patterns of behaviour you're trying to form in your kids or the 'strategies' for family life that you forget to dig the foundation, you forget to build your relationship with God (see chapter thirteen). Your choices as far as strategies are concerned may differ from mine, you might use corporal punishment, I may find it inappropriate, you might loathe the idea of a star-chart, I may find it very effective. None of this matters half so much as we think it does. What matters most of all is that all of us base our lives and our homes on God's unconditional love of us and find our own appropriate ways of expressing that same kind of love to everyone else in our family.

CHAPTER SEVEN

Anger:
When You Find Yourself Shouting

All children get angry. Unless you are extremely naïve or have very little to do with children, this statement will not come as any great surprise. They are, after all, the little guys and life does not always cooperate with them. Their anger tends to peak at those stages of life where their desire to get on with things is hampered by their lack of ability. For example, a toddler wants desperately to put on his shoes and to do up his own coat but as he hasn't yet mastered the necessary physical skills, so he copes with his frustration by flatly refusing to wear either. Similarly a teenager usually has 'grown up' aspirations that are a few years in advance of the skills necessary for independence (i.e. they can't drive and they can't earn). This is frustrating for them and suddenly it's tantrum time again.

If you were to run your finger along the Family Life shelf in your library or book-shop you would be likely to find several books on how to tame your toddler's tantrums, handle your child's anger or channel their frustration. The fact that many of these are best-sellers is a strong indication of just how anxious we feel when our children are unruly. However, this chapter will not be going over the ground that such books have already covered, because I am not going to talk about your child's anger but *your* anger. It seems to me that with so much attention focused on our children's very predictable and well-documented anger, the subject of parental anger has been somewhat overlooked. It is assumed that when we read advice such as 'When your child loses his temper, it will help if you stay calm', we will all automatically be able to adopt a calm controlled manner and all will be well. If only life were so simple, if only we parents could be automatically programmed to respond calmly, if only we weren't so . . . well, human really.

This chapter aims to be realistic about the subject of parental anger. I am going to assume that as we *are* all human and emotional beings we will, therefore, experience the emotion of anger in our homes, from time to time. That anger is often provoked by our children and often directed towards our children. What I would like to discuss in this chapter is firstly, how does the experience of God's unconditional love for us help us when we are angry? Secondly, how can we demonstrate that kind of love to our children, even though we are angry?

I love the story about the father in the supermarket who was working his weekly way round the store, bravely ignoring his young son who was having a full-blown tantrum at his side. On hearing this patient father repeating quiet commands such as 'Hush now, George', 'Keep quiet, George' and 'Calm down, George' a lady customer felt moved to congratulate him on his mild response to his son's behaviour.

'I'm sure George will turn out well in the end from having such a patient father,' she said. The man looked at her for a moment and then said, 'I'm George.'[1]

We have all been in situations where we would like to have distanced ourselves from our child's appalling behaviour, situations when it is extremely difficult to keep our cool and situations when, like George in the story, we have to coach ourselves into staying calm. Escorting a tantruming child from a shop or a church service is not an enjoyable experience. It's bad enough when they're simply wailing, but I've heard of some clever ones who will throw in the occasional 'Don't hit me, Mummy!' just to add to the humiliation. If only you could offer excuses or explanations to the bemused bystanders. Apart from the fact that you wouldn't be heard above all the noise, it can sound a bit limp to say, 'He didn't sleep well last night' when you're struggling to restrain a fierce, red, wriggling child who looks anything but tired.

The good news is that you are quite right to distance yourself – it is not necessarily your fault when your child is bad-tempered and belligerent. If he gets out of bed on the wrong side that's his problem. Everyone is entitled to a bad day every now and again and when he has one, it's just a fact of life. It does not necessarily reflect badly on you as a parent.

The 'not so good' news is that although you are not responsible for his behaviour you are responsible for the way you respond to his behaviour. It is this responsibility that these two chapters are going to focus on; your part in the 'close encounters of the angry kind' that happen in your home. Your response to your child's bad behaviour is the only part of the encounter for which God holds you directly responsible. The difficulty for most of us is to know what type of response we should make. Does 'calm' mean 'wishy washy', does 'controlled' mean we should never raise our voice and does 'patient' mean we should never, ever lose our temper? Even when we've decided how we should respond, the main reason why most of us do not respond that way is because our own feeling of anger gets in the way. So let's start by taking a close look at the real reasons for our anger.

WHAT AM I REALLY ANGRY ABOUT?

Helen has just come back on her bike from playing at her friend's house. You remind her that her bike must be put away. The following morning you discover that her bike, which was left leaning up against the shed, instead of securely locked inside it, has been stolen. Your daughter's disobedience, her careless attitude, our crime-ridden society, all of these combine to make you angry. If an 'on the spot' reporter were to suddenly appear at your side and ask you what you were angry about you'd have no difficulty formulating your reply. When our anger is in proportion to the offensive behaviour, it is legitimate (that means, you are allowed to be angry) and it is also appropriate and understandable.

The trouble is there are many occasions when the anger we unleash is out of all proportion to the offensive deed, occasions when we suddenly explode over some minor misdemeanour or when one sullen look or just a question ('When will tea be ready?') can release a torrent of annoyance. If at such a moment that 'on the spot' reporter were to ask the same question 'What are you angry about?' our reply might be a little more complicated. On the surface we might be angry because of the sullen look or the door left open but our over-reaction betrays the fact that there are all sorts of other reasons why we are angry. Many of these reasons may have nothing to do with the child nor be directly related to the offending deed, yet the child or the action have triggered a 'hot spot' into an eruption, to use a volcanic metaphor. I have also heard this phenomenon described as the 'kick the cat' syndrome – in other words, the nearest available and vulnerable object receives the full force of our anger. If only it were more often the cat and less often our kids, less emotional damage would be done in our homes.

How does this syndrome work in practice. It's a

Wednesday morning and it's your turn today on the coffee rota for the Mother and Toddler group. You need to be there by 9.30am. Before you get there you have to drop your older child at school, buy the milk and biscuits, post the letters your husband has left for you to deal with, and go to the bank. Your younger two are unaware of your schedule and see no reason why they shouldn't have a game of hide and seek at 8.50am. Having found them and strapped them firmly into your form of transport, you rush your older child to school. Still complaining loudly, your younger two make your errands three times as hard to get through. It not very surprising that when you arrive late at the toddler group you are feeling angry. You may appear to be angry at your children but are there lots of other people with whom you are also angry? Maybe you are angry with yourself, 'I should have got the milk and biscuits earlier, why am I so disorganised?' Or perhaps it's your husband with whom you are most annoyed, 'Why does he just assume I have time to run his errands for him?' Perhaps you are angry with the other people at the group; 'Why is it my turn again? If only that lot would help on the rota I wouldn't have to do this so often.'

All of these reasons to be angry are floating semi-submerged in your mind. You don't really want to own up to these unpleasant feelings so what actually happens is this: your middle child elbows the baby in the face, the baby yells in protest and you explode like someone setting a match to a fire-cracker. Whoosh! One little deed and you've gone up in smoke. The trigger event was tiny but the response was spectacular. If only that 'on the spot' reporter had come along a few minutes earlier and helped you to voice what you were really angry about, you might not have directed your anger so inappropriately.

It's not always our feelings of anger that trigger an inappropriate response. Sometimes anger is the secondary emotion, the one we use to cover over feelings of guilt or anxiety. The other day my young son came to me in the kitchen and said, 'I'm *starving* for something, Mummy.' This innocent remark made me really annoyed. If he wasn't starving, and I knew he wasn't because he had not long eaten a full dinner followed by his weekly sweet treat, he was bored, it was a sort of 'I don't know what to do next so maybe I'll eat something' request. It didn't warrant the outburst it received. Why was I so cross? Because 'boredom eating' is one of my own personal battlegrounds, and seeing the same trait in one of my kids raised all sorts of guilty feelings. I shrugged off the guilt with anger. On another occasion the 'problem' emotion fuelling your anger could be anxiety: a row breaks out between the kids just after the TV has been turned off. Those moments between passive entertainment and active playing are a fertile time for rows. Your response may not just be an angry one ('Don't poke your sister') but also an anxious one ('I won't let you watch it if this is how you behave') since you may be anxious about the amount or type of television programmes they are watching and this anxiety expresses itself as anger.

We shall come on to consider guilt and anxiety in the next few chapters. For the time being let's concentrate on anger. We can be angry for a whole lot of reasons that go beyond the immediate situation of the home and family. Anger that is allowed to remain unacknowledged has a way of getting stored up inside us until it becomes a core of bitterness. The Bible calls it a 'root of bitterness' (Hebrews 12:15) and this is a useful picture because like a root our hidden away anger spreads out and touches every part of our lives and relationships. We may be bitter about our status, perhaps we'd like a better job, perhaps we resent the unpaid labour of child-care, even if that's what we've 'chosen'. We could be bitter about our income, and this would affect relationships with anyone earning more than us. Maybe we don't like where we live, we feel we need a bigger house. Maybe we feel disappointed in our marriage or bitter about a friend who seems to have let us down. Perhaps we are bitter because our church fellowship doesn't seem to see things our way. When the Bible warns us about a destructive 'root of bitterness' the warning is not just for our fellowships, it is important for our families. We cannot expect to carry around a load of anger and bitterness inside without it affecting us. The fact is that it will cause us to over-react, 'cause trouble and defile many'. And the first of the many will be those in our own homes.

WHAT SHOULD I DO WITH MY ANGER?

The first thing we must do if we want to rid ourselves of this inner core of anger is to actually admit that it is there. Anger is an emotion that makes us feel uncomfortable so we prefer to think of ourselves as 'a bit low', 'needing a change of scenery', 'run down', anything but angry. However, we cannot effectively deal with the emotion that is driving us if we do not own up to the fact that it is there. A little honest self-examination goes a long way: what am I really feeling? When did I start feeling this way? These are good questions that can often lead us back to the trigger event that put us in a bad mood. Maybe a friend has been telling you all about the foreign holiday she has just booked. Instead of sharing her joy, you find yourself wondering when you'll ever be able to afford such a holiday. Perhaps this envy settles down into anger, anger about your status, your income or your inability to do just what you'd like to do. This is a very straightforward example, but self-examination is not always so simple. The Bible tells us that 'the heart is deceitful above all things' (Jeremiah 17:9) but also reassures us that God knows our hearts and knows our thoughts from afar (Psalm 139:2).

So if we are willing to expose our thoughts to him, then he is willing to reveal, through his Holy Spirit, the root cause of our anger. This is not a case of 'eyes closed, head down, you deal with it, Lord, make me a better person and let me know when you've finished'; only painful self-awareness leads to genuine repentance which in turn leads to change.

Some people know only too well the cause of their anger and bitterness but hold on to it all the more tightly. They do this because they think their feelings and demands are justified. They are angry at God for something he hasn't done or at other people for also failing to do the things they think they should do. For example, 'I'm angry that God hasn't given me a job/helped us move house/healed my sister/saved my husband'. Or 'I'm angry at other people, they don't seem to care about me/they let me down/ leave me out/hurt me'. When we feel misunderstood, frustrated, slighted or thwarted and we feel that this situation is through no fault of our own, the soil is fertile for a demanding anger to grow up. We begin to demand of life, of God and of other people that it/they should cooperate to make our lives how we would like them to be: happy, healthy and fulfilled.

The trouble with our demands is that they can often sound so reasonable: 'Surely God intends me to be healthy', 'Surely he can see how much I need a job, hasn't he promised to meet my needs anyway?' The fact is that God will listen with tender compassion to the hurts and disappointments that daily life doles out to us, and he will often mercifully and generously respond to our petitions and requests, but he will not hear us when we stamp our feet and demand. We may be able to make our demand sound like a polite reasonable request, we might even be able to back it up with a verse of scripture, but if we believe that whatever we are demanding is essential to our well-being and happiness then God will not hear us. He will not be replaced. It is a relationship with him that is the one thing necessary for our well-being and happiness. He is the Creator God and he does indeed give us many good things that make us happy (homes, friends, families) but if we place more emphasis on the possession of these gifts than on the possession of a relationship with the Giver, we have seriously misunderstood who we are before God. God is God and we are dependent creatures under his authority, we are not in a position to demand anything. Anger and bitterness are often the emotional clouds generated by unspoken demands about how we'd like life to be. In order to be free of the black clouds we have to uncover our demands and realise that in the presence of God they are unreasonable.

The beginning of a proper response to frustrating circumstances is a clear recognition of who's in charge. To handle frustration by reminding ourself how much God loves us is a good second step, but not the first one. We must take our place as a creature before our Creator and *then* explore the wonder of God's loving character. An awareness of God's love casts out fear, but subjection to His authority deals with our demandingness. (Larry Crabb)[2]

I wrote earlier that God, as our perfect parent, longs to meet those two essential longings of our heart, the longing for significance and the longing for security. If you have been seeking a 'ministry', or a bigger house or a better job as a way of fulfilling these longings then it is likely that God will not have allowed your search to be fruitful. He desires that you know yourself to be unconditionally loved as you are and to be accepted, as you are, on the basis of his acceptance of you. You are significant now by virtue of the fact that you are his child, and you do not need status or success to prove your significance. I'm not saying that it's wrong to desire a job if you are unemployed, of course you should seek work, but when it comes it is a gift and, like all gifts, it is to be used in the service of God. It is not given to serve our sense of self-worth.

Once we've recognised that our anger is a demand, the way to deal with it is to repent. Repentance may be plain, simple and old-fashioned but it is 100 per cent effective. When you pray a prayer of repentance don't say 'God, help me deal with these demanding feelings', but say 'I'm sorry, I repent, I was wrong'. God is not in the business of applying therapy for our problem emotions. He is in the business of forgiving our stubborn sinfulness.

If all this sounds rather 'heavy' and profound for the simple problem of a short temper I would caution you not to gloss over it too quickly. It is not so far removed from the way we relate to our children. If we refuse to take a look inside ourselves and see what is driving us, then any changes of tone or manner on the surface are likely to be cosmetic and short-lived. Only when we've resolved the root causes of our anger can we begin to work on controlling our response to any given situation. Practical suggestions about how we can control our anger will only be of use to you if you have already done the groundwork of understanding yourself.

CHAPTER EIGHT

Anger: Towards Better
Ways of Communication

'Out! Out! Get out, you stupid thing!'

My children looked at me with subdued surprise and mild concern. They'd been summoned into the kitchen to wash their hands before tea. My remarks weren't addressed to them. I was talking to the lasagna. Well, shrieking at it would be a more precise description.

With the benefit of hindsight I can see that I had not picked the best day for cooking mass quantities of lasagna. One of the kids was off school sick and I was still suffering exhaustion, the after-effect of a heavy cold. It had been a boiling hot day and the fruit of all my labours (two trays of lasagna) had just got burnt because requests for juice and entertainment had distracted me for a critical ten minutes. Yes, our oven does have a timer device, don't ask me why I didn't set it. David came in from work, sniffed the air and asked just that question. My reply was less than polite! Tiredness, hunger, irritation, disappointment, and frustration all reached a peak when the wretched lasagna refused to part company with the baking dish. It was at this point that I shrieked at it.

Truly anger is a complicated emotion! Even when you understand all the factors that have conspired to aggravate you it doesn't really help. Shouting at an innocent dish of lasagna may seem completely illogical but at least I was unlikely to hurt its feelings. I was really shouting at myself, as I tried to explain to David when he came to take over the task of dishing up tea. He listened very patiently for someone who is now an expert at scraping off the burnt bits. Love is a husband who attends to your disasters while you sob on the sofa and who doesn't let you see the 'creation' until it's presentable!

The burnt lasagna had been the last straw for me that afternoon, but what if a comment from one of the children had been the last straw? Would I have been justified in shouting at them? How should I handle my anger when it relates to my children? Is it wrong to shout?

'Stay calm' never seemed to me to be a very helpful definition of what to do when you are angry. Does it mean always speaking with a smile on your face or always speaking softly? Does it mean never feeling angry? Is there a way that I can communicate my angry feelings without being destructive? I have to accept the fact that I will feel angry, so I need a better definition of what kind of response I'm going to make when I am angry. If I don't define it, I'll never achieve it.

My definition of the response I try to make in any situation where I am angry is this: it should be **responsible** and **respectful**. By **responsible** I mean that I am taking responsibility for my own feelings. I will keep short accounts of how I am feeling and if there are other feelings fuelling my anger (tiredness, anxiety) I will take responsibility for these and be careful not to lay the blame for all these feelings on my child. Depending on the age of my child it may be appropriate to tell them how I am feeling. This is usually more effective said in advance of any potential quarrel, not after the event when it can sound as if you are offering excuses. I had already done this on the day of the lasagna bake-in, so when I got upset the kids knew in advance it wasn't all their fault. However, telling them I was poorly did not give me permission to lay all the blame at their door when they distracted me. I could not make them responsible for my problems. My aim is to simply be responsibly aware of all the factors influencing me at any moment. Part of being **responsible** lies in thinking ahead. If rows occur with sickening regularity at the same time of day (before school, at bedtime), then it makes sense to take steps to relieve yourself of as many stress-inducing factors that you can influence (make the lunch boxes the night before, unplug the phone). We usually lose our temper over a cumulation of little things, 'like being stoned to death with marbles,'[1] so take responsibility to change as many of the 'little things' you can.

However, you cannot reorganise a situation in such a way as to completely eliminate stress, so there will always be plenty of scope for the exercise of self-control. Self-control is the essence of responsibility. As self-control is a fruit of the Spirit and a gift of God (Galatians 5: 22 and 2 Timothy 1: 7) that makes it, by my reckoning, something I have to depend on God for. It's something I need to pray for in my waking moments, through the day and in the heat of the rows. This is what I mean by making a **responsible** response.

By **respectful** I mean that my response should not demean or humiliate the person to whom I am expressing my anger. It should be an expression that does not denigrate their value as a person. Whatever they have done (ignored me, disobeyed me) has made me angry because it has undermined my value (I feel used or rejected), but because I am affirmed by God I do not have to respond in a way that undermines their value. No matter how irritating their behaviour as people they are still unique and precious individuals. If being responsible is measured by your level of self-control then being respectful is measured by what you say and how you say it. Let's look at these in reverse order.

HOW YOU SAY IT

Some families seem so calm and dignified, so cheerful and chummy that you can't ever imagine them arguing. We must comfort ourselves with the fact that such families are rare and possibly even unhealthy. The reality is that every family has its rows and arguments; most of us shout a bit, some of us shout a lot, but all of us have a snapping point. Our snapping point is usually fairly near the end of a scale of possible responses. For example, suppose shoes are left lying all over the stairs. First of all we might ignore the offence ('I shall tidy these away but if it happens again . . .'), or we might store the offence until we have a stock-pile of grievances ('That's the third time I've had to ask you to move these'), then if we don't like confrontation we may try to avoid it with some dishonest remark ('I guess it doesn't matter, I shouldn't have expected you to do it'). Finally when we reach the end of the scale we explode and the explosion is often ineffectual ('Why am I the only one around here who clears up?'). Just as we are thinking 'this is annoying but I'm handling it' we 'snap' and lose control. If we'd had time to hear the thought that passed through our mind just before we snapped we'd have heard something like, 'I've had enough of this aggravation, now I'm going to throw my weight around'. The verbal outcome of this thought process is usually 'I've had it up to here with you lot, now just listen . . .' or 'Right, that does it . . .' Sound familiar?

So is it okay to shout? Well, there are different sorts of shouting. There's the '*Stop*!' (before the kerb) type of shouting, when your child must know that your tone implies that instant obedience is imperative for his safety. Then there's the 'Oi, come over here' type of shouting, useful for large gardens, people with loft extensions and outings to the park. The more unpleasant varieties are the sudden 'Let's get some action around here' shouting that demands quick obedience but omits any prior explanations or warnings. Then there's the 'wearied whine' style of shouting (otherwise known as nagging), 'Oh, come *on*'. There's also the 'what the heck' style of shouting, I've been shouting all day I may as well shout some more. And finally there's the full blown 'I don't deserve this kind of treatment' adult version of a tantrum.

As you can probably tell, I've tried 'em all! The difficulty is to know what is reasonable and acceptable and what's destructive. When my daughter leaves a piece of toast on the kitchen floor (don't ask why) and then proceeds to skid on it across the full length of the floor, sending crockery and siblings flying, then, yes, I do think that for me to shout is not only understandable, it's also perfectly reasonable.

'All things in moderation' isn't just a guide for sensible eating. It also works well as a guide to sensible shouting. If you live in a house where voices are rarely, if ever, raised and when they are, everyone feels extremely uncomfortable, then it's worth asking yourself, are you allowing yourself and your children the right to own and express negative feelings and emotions? If family members disagree about something and the disagreement only results in distant silence and hidden resentment, nothing is solved and children learn that 'keeping the peace' is more important than resolving the problems.

Far better to live in a home where children and adults are allowed to say how they feel, are allowed to disagree. This is rarely destructive providing it is done in an atmosphere of respect, and providing that reconciliation is a regular routine that naturally follows any outburst of strong feelings. As adults we need to be learning how to express our anger and other bad feelings in a way that is not destructive, offensive or humiliating.

Maybe you feel your home is at the other extreme,

you feel you are shouting or being shouted at all day long. Rows, confrontation and arguments have become the norm and the atmosphere is always tense. If so, it's time to step back and assess the situation. I don't want to send you on a guilt trip by reminding you that you are the only one who can change, because I do not mean to imply that the situation is all your fault, just that you are the one who can make a difference. Nor do I want you to get too hung up about those occasional 'off days' when you are short-tempered. Everyone has those. On the other hand, if you take an objective view of the family and it appears that angry rows and constant confrontations have become the norm, then it's time to change things.

Understanding is always at the beginning of change. I have found David Augsburger's definition of anger a real help in understanding the problem of anger. In his book *Caring enough to Confront*, he describes anger as 'a self-affirming emotion which responds reflexively to the threat of rejection or devaluation with the messages (1) I am a person, a precious person and (2) I demand that you recognise and respect me.'[2] He goes on to say that anger is a demand 'that you recognise my worth'. In other words when I feel that another person is about to engulf me or incorporate me (assuming ownership of me, taking me for granted, using me, absorbing me in his or her life-program), I feel angry. So if you feel the sole reason for your anger is your child's bad behaviour, think again. It isn't just his bad behaviour in itself that is annoying, it is the effect his bad behaviour has on you. There are few people in your life better qualified to assume ownership of you, few people who are better placed to take you for granted, to use you, to 'absorb you' than your kids. No wonder you feel so angry! The danger of 'self-affirming' anger is that we affirm *our* rights at the expense of the other person's rights, we raise our self-respect by tearing them down. The key to effective control and expression of anger is knowing that God affirms me, he knows that I am precious, he recognises and respects me. It is the knowledge of this affirmation that strengthens me to handle all the slights and rejections that my offspring may hand out to me as they grow towards the independence that is adulthood.

It does seem unfair that some of us just do seem to lose our temper more easily than others. I used to have such a bad temper as a teenager that I earned myself a reputation for it. The disappearance of my explosive temper was one of the first noticeable differences in my life after I became a Christian. For a whole decade I firmly believed I no longer had a problem with my temper . . . and then I had kids! The early years of parenthood are often a time when it's very hard to keep your temper, not just because you're often very tired and exhausted but also because small children can be maddening at times. Their behaviour can humiliate you or obstruct you, and you cannot walk away from them. The other problem is that from birth children treat us like objects. This isn't their fault. Their survival depends on it: a baby has to know how to summon the 'milk object' and that 'milk object' has to get out of bed or put down her task to provide milk. It often takes two or three years for it to dawn on the average child that Mum and Dad are not objects. The danger for Mum and Dad is that they will feel so used and mistreated that they will slip into a settled pattern of responding to the child as if it, too, were an object, not a human being whose choices and feelings deserve respect. Our children's demands threaten our worth and the danger is that I will respond without respect for their worth.

'The real menace in dealing with a five year old is that in no time at all you begin to sound like a five year old.'[3]

Children will often say terrible things like 'You're stupid' or 'I hate you' without any understanding of the awfulness of what they are saying. If we find ourselves tempted at moments like these to reply 'You're the one that's stupid' or 'I hate you too' we really need to bite our tongue and remind ourselves that we are the adults and they are the children. We are to set an example in our response. The guidelines for that example are that it should be responsible and respectful, and that it should demonstrate self-control, respect and unconditional love.

Of these three qualities self-control is probably the hardest to implement. The trouble with self-control is that we least want it at the very times we most need it. When every fibre of my being is insisting loudly that it needs the comfort of a cream doughnut the exercise of self-control is a very difficult and unpopular measure! It's the same with anger. When you are on the verge of losing your temper you feel fully justified in what you are about to do. In such circumstances the best demonstration of self-control may be to remove yourself from the scene as fast as possible. You may need to confine the child in some way for its own safety, depending on its age (notice how he or she becomes an 'it' when we are angry with them!). I recommend going to the furthest corner of the house (or garden, depending on how well you know your neighbours) and working out your anger in private. From experience I've learnt that grabbing a crushable grocery item from the vegetable rack and heading for the nearest brick wall is the cheapest option. I've tried hitting things with my bare hands and found out that I could karate chop a waste bin into two halves without ever having been trained, but it hurt! On another occasion I laid into the kitchen floor with a saucepan. Although this was immensely satisfying, it resulted in a permanently misshapen pan. And let me warn you about plastic – if you throw a plastic chair across a room it will break and when it breaks you will then have the humiliation of having to apologise to your child for breaking their chair. I'm not telling you this as some form of confessional. I am telling you so that you will know you are not being lectured about self-control by someone who never needed to learn it herself.

In the end I committed myself to learning self-control for the purely pragmatic reason that retreat and persuade worked better than advance and confront. Remember the fable of the Sun and Wind? They competed with each other to see who could make the traveller remove his cloak? The wind tried to blow the cloak away but the man held on to it all the more tightly. Then the sun shone its warmth on the man and within moments he had removed his cloak. Noisy force almost always backs people into a corner whereas gentle persuasion is more likely to win them round – and this isn't just the stuff of fables; we are wisely advised in the book of Proverbs that a gentle answer turns away wrath (Proverbs 15:1). In order to take this on board we have to give up the notion that we have a 'right' to uncontrolled expression of our feelings. Our explosions of anger and shouted frustrations are more often a form of self-indulgence, not self-expression, and we shoot ourselves in the foot because we only have to make up for these outbursts afterwards.

There is another notion that we also need to give up – the notion that we *always* have to confront. Some books about disciplining children have laid such heavy stress on the 'need' to confront any act of deliberate disobedience and to win that confrontation that they leave the impression that confrontation is our only choice and we would be failing somehow if we failed to confront. The fact is we do *not* always have to confront. There is no harm, for example, in delaying the 'confrontation' until such a time when the feelings over the bad behaviour will have cooled sufficiently to allow for a responsible and respectful discussion (on your part, at least, for you cannot take responsibility for how they might react to your correction). Another verse from Proverbs confirms this, 'It is to a man's honour to avoid strife, but every fool is quick to quarrel' (Proverbs 20:3). When we commit ourselves to constant confrontation we become reactionaries, we are always reacting to situations instead of shaping situations and this leaves us at the mercy of how our children choose to behave. We do not have to react. If self-control is going to characterise the 'how' of our response we must give up our commitment to confrontation.

It is often the daily drudgery of life that makes us forget that our words and actions are shaping our children's lives. This poem by Susan Lenzkes expresses just this fact.

Important Circles

Lord, sometimes I resent
being like a clock
going round in circles
hour after hour,
all day long,
week after week,
doing the same thing.

Help me to remember how
everyone in this house
looks up to that clock
every few minutes
all day long,
week after week.[4]

This poem speaks so clearly of the powerful influence of our seemingly insignificant role. There are often times when we feel our lives go round and round with the hands of the clock or are relentlessly repetitive like the clothes in the washing machine. As I thought about this poem I realised that although I could not set the time for my family, I was responsible for setting the tone. It's worth asking yourself: 'Who sets the tone in my household?' Is it set by the high-pitched self-interested squabbling of the kids or is it dominated by the weary, irritated tones of the adults? Tune into the tone of the way people speak to one another and realise that you are responsible for your contribution to that tone and can in some measure alter it.

'Tone' is a description of sound that tells you about its quality irrespective of its volume. When we are talking about 'tone', rules like 'never shout' are no use, tone is far more than the loudness or softness of your voice. Your tone can be altered by changing what you say and how you say it. I ought to warn you in advance that if you commit yourself to a new way of responding and communicating with your children it will, at first, feel very mechanical, deliberate and self-conscious. But if you practise, responding in a responsible and respectful way will eventually become 'second nature'. For some parents, becoming responsible and respectful will mean that they must become more assertive, more able to express respect for their own needs and not allow their children to use them. But for most parents, especially those with a problem with anger, becoming responsible and respectful will mean learning self-control and altering their words and tone to express respect. Any changes you make will, at first, feel 'unnatural'. It will feel 'forced' to speak as calmly and gently as you can when you are seething with anger inside, but you can remind yourself that letting out all that anger on an already fraught situation will not improve it. By all means 'vent', but not on the child. Allowing the child to provoke you to uncontrolled anger is like handing over a remote control device to your child. He can learn to press the buttons and watch Mummy or Daddy explode whenever he chooses.

Venting your anger on your child might feel good in the short term but it will not contribute to the scaling down of hostilities, and some children will feed off your reaction; in other words the more you react, the more they will persist. You might feel silly cheer-leading your small child round a shopping trip or coaxing him through the dressing routine whilst inside your patience is wearing thin, but in the end a cheerful, Joyce Grenfell-style, nanny tone of voice that assumes obedience is likely to be forthcoming will get you further than nagging or harassing.

CHANGING WHAT YOU SAY

These ground rules for what we should actually say when we are angry have been gleaned from a variety of sources and I have found them all to be extremely effective.[5]

1) Focus on the child's behaviour not on the child's personality. When carelessness leads to an avoidable accident saying 'You stupid child' is ten times more aggressive and personally offensive than 'That was a stupid thing to do'.

2) Express your anger with positive 'I' statements not explosive 'You' statements. Compare these two remarks:

'I feel hurt when you speak so aggressively.'

'You're so rude and arrogant, how dare you speak to me like that.'

The fact that the second remark rolls off the tongue so much more easily than the first is an indication of how we go on the attack when an action makes us feel undermined or threatened. It makes us feel vulnerable to express our feelings (I feel hurt, I feel disappointed) so we prefer to go on the attack (you're so insensitive, you let me down). But being vulnerable is far more effective in terms of resolving the situation. 'You' statements attack, devalue, criticise, and disrespect the other person. 'I' statements are a clear, honest way of owning your own feelings.

3) Simplify your speech: say what you want in the shortest, simplest words you can find. Do not overload a request with sarcasm. 'Please would you hang your coat up' is simple and direct whereas 'I suppose you think those coats will just fly up on the pegs' is sarcastic, demeaning and aggressive. Speak honestly, not manipulatively. 'Why do I always have to ask twice for help around here?' loads guilt on to the listener and states as fact that they 'never' help. 'When are you going to do something about the mess you've left in the kitchen?' is a question that manages to sneak in a moan and a command and, because it devalues your teenager, it is more likely to be ignored than a more respectful expression such as 'I feel very discouraged when I come to prepare a meal and find the kitchen left untidy. I feel frustrated that I have to clear away before I can cook, so if you cannot leave the kitchen tidy I will not allow you to use it.' (It helps to recognise that the mess in the kitchen is not a problem for them. It is a problem for you and they need to learn consideration for your problems. If, however, the mess is in *their* bedroom, it can be *their* problem. It need not be a problem for you, all you need to do is learn to shut the door!)

4) Use questions with care: 'Why?' is a very aggressive question that closes down many a discussion before it gets going. Asking why puts you in the role of interrogator/ accuser and them in the defendant's box. Of course, you will have to use a why question occasionally but see how far you can get with 'what' and 'how' questions first.

5) Reaffirm the child at the end of any row. You are not angry with the child but with his behaviour. Reminding him that you love him and think he's a great kid will help him to focus on what he did wrong rather than the row he got for it. (More on this in chapter ten on guilt).

Communication is a two-way thing. If we are trying to move towards better ways of communicating, we must try to change not only what we say and how we say it, but also change the way we hear. It is, of course, anatomically impossible to hear with anything other than our ears but as parents our ears can often feel worn out and over-loaded with requests, interruptions and blow by blow commentaries on life, not to mention the squabbling and wailing. 'It's not fair', 'You said I could', 'Can I have a . . .', 'Please, Mum, please', 'Where's my . . .?'

One day my husband, who is a scientist, brought home a little device from work. It was called a 'personal exposure-to-sound meter'. I immediately volunteered as subject matter for research! From the moment we wake until we fall asleep our ears are on duty, monitoring the sound levels in our home. We cannot even enjoy the 'peace and quiet' if they are quiet because 'they must be up to something'. Because we cannot turn our ears off we develop a defence mechanism called 'selective deafness'. This is especially useful at night when it ensures your partner has to attend to the wakeful child. By the time our children are articulate enough to actually express meaningful opinions, many of us have been so bombarded with sound that we need to re-learn how to listen, and this is what I mean by changing the way we hear.

Remember we are aiming to demonstrate responsibility and respect. If what we say and how we say it is largely a demonstration of responsibility, then learning to listen effectively is the best way of communicating respect. A child who feels listened to will also feel accepted, respected and loved unconditionally.

Sadly the emphasis on reaction and confrontation in many books about child-rearing has meant that the value of listening has been underplayed. Drawing greatly on the work of Dr Thomas Gordon, Michael and Terri Quinn, authors of the excellent parenting course, *What can a Parent do?*,[6] describe active listening as holding up a mirror to your child's feelings. This is what I mean by choosing to reflect rather than react. The art of active listening lies in helping the child to understand his own feelings better and to express them more clearly. At the same time you gain a better understanding of your child.

Imagine the following: your two boys, we'll call them Tim and Jonathan, have just come home from school. They usually walk home together but they come in separately and when the younger one comes in he bangs the back door, throws down his bag and says, 'I hate Jonathan.' If you were locked into reacting mode you might see this statement as a defiant, undesirable attitude and move at once to confront it: 'It's wrong to hate people Tim, go to your room until you are ready to apologise.' There are several problems with this sort of reaction. First, you've shut down the conversation instantly. Secondly, you've stifled the expression of a strong emotion. Thirdly, you've failed to demonstrate any respect or love for Tim: he is labelled as being wrong before anyone has made an effort to understand him. Active listening does not require you to confront; instead it gives you the choice to reflect. You can hold up a mirror to your child's feelings with a remark like, 'You feel very angry with your brother, Tim?' This is far more likely to open up the conversation, and he might reply with, 'Yes, he let me get the blame for something I didn't do.' Children are capable of working out what's right and wrong; we do not have to dole out hasty judgements. Your aim is not to get entangled in their argument and take sides but instead to help them articulate the problem and work towards their own solution. Try remarks that reflect, that play back the feelings; sound out what you think you are hearing and allow the child to agree or disagree with your impressions: 'you seem to be feeling . . .', 'it sounds as if . . .'.

Children often don't have the words to articulate their feelings. When my four-year-old said she 'hated' a close family friend I was appalled, but when I explored how she had come to feel that way it turned out that her real feeling was one of embarrassment at having been told off (albeit appropriately) by this person. What she needed from me was understanding, not further confrontation. We so want our children to conform to Christian standards of behaviour that sometimes we leap in to react and correct undesirable behaviours without stopping to understand, and without respecting our children's ability to choose these behaviours and attitudes for themselves.

Dr Ross Campbell gives helpful advice about active listening in his book *How to really love your child*,[7] referring to it as 'focused attention': giving your child your whole attention, 'listening' with your expression, through eye contact, through appropriate touch. Clearly it is not possible to do this all day long, every day, but he recommends that each of your children be given a daily period of focused attention. This suggestion, like some of the others I've covered, is preventative and it will go a long way towards lowering the tension levels in your home. The other suggestions that I've made in this chapter are more about how to behave in the heat of a disagreement. None of these suggestions will make much difference if you are not prepared to look inside at whatever else might be fuelling your anger.

The presence of uncontrolled anger in your home could very often be motivated by feelings of guilt, even if it is not so motivated the destructive expression of anger can leave a stain of guilt on your life.

CHAPTER NINE

Guilt:
'Maybe I've Done This All Wrong'

It's late in the evening. The children have been in bed for a couple of hours and you are heading that way yourself. As you are pottering in and out of their rooms delivering piles of clean clothes and restoring toys to their original owners, you stop to gaze at their sleepy faces. Today they took it in turns to fight each other and fight you. You nagged them through tea and then hurried them into bed, too weary to take time over a story or prayers. All you could think about was being able to sit down with a soothing cup of tea and watch some undemanding television. Now, late at night, as you look at their tousled heads and relaxed faces, you think how small they are. It's so easy to forget how young they are. When they pit their wills against you they can seem so much older. How is it they can look so lovely when they are asleep and yet be so stroppy during the day? You started out this morning with so much hopeful resolve that you'd get along today, that there wouldn't be rows. Will tomorrow be any better? You find yourself thinking, 'Why is parenthood such hard going? Do other parents find it so hard? Maybe it's just me? Perhaps I'm just getting it all wrong.'

How do we cope as parents with that vague inner feeling of guilt and uncertainty: 'Maybe I've done this all wrong',

'Maybe I've failed as a parent', 'Perhaps it's too late to change'.

I'd like you to picture for a moment the feeling of guilt as if it were a signal from a radio mast. Think back over the previous few days and imagine that a small mast was set up on each occasion when you were unreasonable, inconsistent or unloving. In other words think back over every little failing of the last few days and try to tune in to the 'guilty' message that each event may still be sending you. Think back still further and see if you can recall the regrets, mistakes or missed opportunities of the last few weeks. Are you still picking up a radio signal from the masts erected at the sites of those 'failures'? If you were to think back still further over the years, would there still be masts beaming messages of guilt and failure at you from events that took place a long time ago? If all these masts are left unattended, each one will send out its own message in a sort of emotional Morse code: 'You're a failure', 'You're too selfish to be a good mother', 'You only ever have time to tell your kids off'. All of these signals have the power to affect us. If your emotions are sensitively tuned into these feelings, all you will be able to hear is the 'misery blues' with lyrics such as 'I've done it all so wrong, so often, I may as well give up'. You can be sure that if you listen to this tune long enough it will take hold of your emotions and drive your behaviour. Even if you are not sensitively tuned in to these signals, they may still be strong enough to cause a lot of noisy interference over your emotional airwaves, causing confusion and uncertainty about the right choices to make for your child.

The trouble with these signals from the distant and recent past is that they are extremely unreliable. Sometimes we deserve to feel guilty and sometimes we don't. So how much attention should we pay to them? Some parents pay them a lot of attention, and they worry endlessly about whether they have given enough time to their kids, whether they've made the right choices for them, whether they've let them down. If their child has a distressing experience they hold themselves on a 'guilty' charge even if they were powerless over what happened. If they allowed the evidence to be examined they might actually get a 'not guilty' verdict, but because they *feel* so guilty, they assume they are.

Then there is a second group of parents who, knowing all these guilty signals are notoriously unreliable, attempt to ignore them altogether. They rarely question themselves, and see it as a virtue to have a 'no regrets' policy. It would be very hard for them to ever admit they might have been wrong. Certainly they are free from all that noisy interference over the airwaves but only because they've switched off their receiver.

I suspect that only a small number of parents fall into either of these two groups that I've described. The rest of us form a third group. We receive the guilty messages but we don't tune in to them. We're not really listening nor do we make any effort to be rid of these signals, so they form a background buzz of interference. Guilt creates a low level of confusion and uncertainty: 'Am I a good parent?', 'Have I made the right choices?'

Switching off our emotional receiver is one way to eliminate unnerving uncertainty but it is not the best way. A certain amount of uncertainty is good for us since it keeps us from being arrogant. If we thought that we had parenthood 'sussed', what point would there be in depending on an all-knowing, all wise God? No, we certainly should not try to block out guilt feelings. Guilt performs a function – it has a message for us. We need to allow that message to be heard but we also need to learn how to interpret it. We do not have to tolerate the constant crackle of interference or the 'misery blues' being played over our emotional airwaves. Instead we can interpret these unreliable signals by examining the evidence. We must do this, otherwise guilt will take hold of our emotions and drive our behaviour. The main skill of interpreting is learning to tell the difference between deserved guilt and false guilt.

We must aim to answer two questions, 'Where does guilt come from?' and 'How can I recognise false guilt?' By answering these questions we should be able to dismiss the feelings of false guilt. That will leave us with just the feeling of valid guilt to contend with in the next chapter, when we shall also explore how the nature of God's accepting love can set us free from the guilt we feel we deserve because of our past mistakes and regrets. Finally we'll look at practical ways of keeping our homes and lives free from the disabling emotion of guilt.

WHERE DOES GUILT COME FROM?

If I had to design a badge of office for parents to wear I'm not sure I'd be able to choose a suitable emblem, as most images of parenthood relate only to the early years, things like nappy pins and potties. However I'd have no difficult in choosing a motto. I'd crib it from Charles Dickens and have the words 'Great Expectations' engraved under the emblem. These words seem to sum up what it feels like to be a parent today. Society has great expectations of us as parents: we are not just expected to feed, clothe and clean our offspring, we are also expected to nurture, educate and guide our children towards being a model of good citizenship. Parents are blamed for many of society's ills yet at the same time family life is eroded and undermined financially and morally by society itself.

It is certainly true that there are 'great expectations' placed upon us by society at large. Our desire and/or failure to live up to these expectations is one source of guilt, but it is not the only one. We also have great expectations of ourselves. If you don't believe me sit down and write a job description of all that you do as a parent. You will realise that the very nature of your job as a parent sets you up for guilty feelings. This is because it carries a huge amount of responsibility, and the level of guilt we are capable of feeling over any task rises in line with the level of responsibility we have for that task.

Say, for example, you have organised a day at the seaside for a group of friends and it all goes wrong. The train is late, you forget the sandwiches, it pours with rain and the amusement park is closed. You would probably feel very guilty even though not all the disasters were your fault. If, however, you had just been invited on the day out you might feel angry, wet and hungry but you're unlikely to feel guilty, because you had no responsibility for the day's events. When you apply this principle to parenthood you'll realise that as a parent you have an immense capacity to feel guilt because you have an immense responsibility. You were responsible for bringing your child into the world, and now you are responsible for providing for your child's every need, physical, emotional and spiritual, knowing that your nurture and example will radically affect the course of your child's life. What a responsibility! Thinking about it too often can make us feel like resigning. There are so many areas where we can make mistakes and receive so much conflicting advice that it all adds up to a huge potential for guilt.

As if that isn't enough some people, especially Christians, have an enlarged sense of responsibility. Instead of just taking responsibility for their lives, they take responsibility for their whole world. On the surface the way they behave may appear very 'Christian' since they meet other people's needs without being asked, they always put other people first, they are people who 'cope', people who excel at 'looking after'. The problem is that these people are driven by an 'ought to' mentality. They feel awkward and uncomfortable in the presence of someone else's problem and they feel they 'ought to' do something. This 'ought to' reflex is not in fact motivated by Christian love but by a sense of guilt and low self-esteem. When we 'rescue' other people from their problems it gives us the pleasant feeling of being more competent than they are and it makes us feel needed. The problem arises when we need to feel needed in order to feel accepted: 'We don't feel lovable, so we settle for being needed!'[1]

This sort of 'love' for people quickly runs out when we feel we've been put upon once too often. We feel angry and resentful but because we're so 'nice' and so good at 'coping' we carry on saying 'yes' when we mean 'no'. We do things for people that they are capable of doing for themselves and this is the heart of the problem of over-responsibility: people who are over-responsible (the technical term is co-dependent) rescue other people from *their* responsibilities. In fact all of us can only be responsible for our own lives and not for any one else's. (Obviously in the case of children we have a degree of responsibility for their actions and choices but even this responsibility is given to us by God and we do not seek it for ourselves.)

Here's a little do-it-yourself test that you can try to see if you suffer from the problem of over-responsibility: your mother is always asking you to visit her, your neighbour is always asking you to fetch her shopping, your friend is always asking you to visit her or have her kids for her. Do you start out on these chores full of saintly pride but, after a few weeks, find that you are a boiling cauldron of resentment? Why do you feel this way when you had meant to be so loving? Why? Because you respected their feelings and 'needs' as being more important than your feelings and needs. While your needs and desires are always placed at the bottom of the pile you'll never live your own life, instead you'll live life running and fetching and sorting for other people. We should not disrespect ourselves in this way. Jesus said we are to 'love our neighbour as ourselves' (Matt 22:39). We are to go the extra mile *when* we are asked, not because we feel we 'ought to'. The 'ought to' mentality leads to a choiceless driven kind of love that leaves us feeling used and exhausted. If we really want to relate lovingly to people we must deflate our enlarged sense of responsibility. Your Mum will not develop her own circle of friends while she depends on you. If your neighbour can make it to bingo every week the chances are she can cope with getting the few things you regularly have to fetch for her from the local shop. Your friend has other people she can ask to have her kids and if she respects you she will not feel rejected by your 'no'. If you always say 'yes' the resentment you will be left with will not enhance the relationship.

All this is difficult territory for some people since they envisage a 'brave new world' of self-interested Christians. That is not what I am advocating at all. Of course we should reach out in love to other people, but let's make sure it *is* out of love not out of guilt or a need to be needed. In the Christian community there are far too many people, women especially, whose lives are driven by the needs of those around them. The antidote to this is a dose of truth: God loves you because of who you are – his child – not because of what you do. You can only be responsible for living your own life. You are not God's sole rescue agent in your part of the world. People with problems need more of God, not more of you. A need expressed is not the same thing as a call to action.

How did Jesus cope with the huge needs all around him? He only said and did that which he saw his Father in Heaven would have him do (John 8: 28, 29). If we are running ourselves ragged at the expense of our marriage or our family we must ask, 'Have I actually been called to do this?' God's yoke is 'easy', that doesn't mean it's not hard work, but it fits and he gives the vision and strength for the task. The primary task we have been given is to maintain our marriages and care for our children; responsibility in any other direction is going to require careful accounting of our time and energy.

So guilt comes from without, from the 'great expectations' that society has of us, but it also comes from within, from the great expectations we have of ourselves. Our inner expectations are at a peak when we first become parents, so let's now turn our attention to the first area where we are vulnerable to false guilt.

THE EARLY YEARS

It is possible for you to be swamped by guilt from the very first moment of parenthood. Maybe you read up on every possible way to give birth while you were pregnant. Naturally you wanted to give your baby the best possible start in life but high expectations are rarely fulfilled. You could have been left with a feeling of guilt because you didn't give birth standing up, whilst reciting nursery rhymes backwards, all without the aid of pain-killing drugs. If the birth went okay there is still plenty of scope for failure and guilt during those first few days: you are expected to 'bond', establish breast-feeding, gently introduce your older child to his rival, receive your visitors with grace and write joyous announcement cards. All this at a time when you feel totally exhausted, tender and decidedly wobbly.

Let's start at the beginning. Giving birth is a process, it is not a performance. The most important thing about a process is its outcome. A healthy child and a reasonably intact, if slightly re-shapen, mother is about the best that anyone can hope for. If you view it as a performance then you will rate your 'success' on how athletic you were, how few stitches you had or how dignified you remained. This is a dangerous way of thinking. I don't mean to put anyone off ante-natal groups or exercises, by all means practise whatever you feel will leave you and the baby in better shape afterwards, but don't place too much emphasis on having your expectations met. You are only a part of the birth process, you are not in charge, so don't take responsibility for factors that are beyond your control. If you do, you invite failure and with it the feeling of guilt.

Once you've got through the birth there are two more guilt traps set to ensnare you on the road ahead: bonding and breast-feeding. The first few weeks of parenthood are not only a test of physical endurance, they are also a time for huge emotional adjustments: you suddenly have no time to yourself, you have to adjust to the baby's affect on your marriage, you have to adjust to yourself physically, and all this on very little sleep. Little wonder then that you may not have found yourself overwhelmed with loving, tender feelings towards this wailing, puking and demanding infant. If you still feel guilty now about the way you felt towards little Joe or Susie during those first few weeks remind yourself that you could not in those circumstances be responsible for the way you were feeling about them since those feelings were beyond your control. What you were responsible for was the way you cared for Joe or Susie. Look at them now. They 'survived' infancy, so did you. By all means pray for them, with someone else if possible, that they may be cut off from any feeling of rejection you had in those early days. Having done this, let yourself off the hook. What matters is how you feel about them now, how you respond to them now. Let go of the guilt from the past.

Breast-feeding is a similar issue. For some women it is

a physical impossibility, others feel extremely uncomfortable about the whole idea. Others of us feel hugely positive about it but have babies who seem to regard it as absurd. If such a fussy feeding infant arrives on the scene just as your toddler is reaching the peak of the 'terrible twos' your chances of successfully feeding her are drastically reduced. Accept that there are many factors that influence how you choose to feed your child, accept also that you do not have control over all of these factors. It can seem to guilt-stricken mothers that research has linked bottle-fed babies to all kinds of undesirable behaviour, ranging from criminal tendencies to learning difficulties. Nonsense! There are 101 other things that will have a far greater influence on your child's life than whether or not you breast-fed him. Nor does it matter very much how, or when, you potty-trained him. Nor will it matter greatly whether you prepared his every meal by hand or boiled some water and opened a packet. Nor, dare I say it, will it matter much whether or not he had a dummy. He's unlikely to still need it when he leaves home at 18, weighing 12 stone, wearing his size 11 shoes.

You can be sure that none of these issues, all hotly debated by baby magazines, will seem half so important then as they do during those early years. The single most important thing during the early years of parenthood is your sanity. If you can turn out mini home-made vegetable terrines without so much as a ripple of stress, fine, go right ahead. If on the other hand you are exhausting yourself and getting into a state trying to purée your baby's every mouthful, give up. Relax, open a packet, sit down and spoon it in and make the most of the chance for lots of eye contact and baby talk. The one thing that a baby needs is its mother and the saner the better! Don't set yourself idealistic goals because there are too many factors in parenting that you can't control.

My first-born never had a dummy and I was terribly

smug about this. My second child humbled me. He had one before he was one week old and its arrival was a great relief to all of us! Unfortunately, he outgrew its soothing effect and at 10 months, on the advice of our Christian family doctor, I agreed to give him a course of nightly sedation. Such a thing would have horrified me the first time round but I was so exhausted and so overwrought that my sanity was seriously at risk. We all know we shouldn't do things 'just to get some peace' but we all need a certain amount of peace, rest and personal space and it's a wise parent who knows their limitations. So make the most of grannies, friends or sisters who'll take them off your hands for a while. If it enables you to give them better quality care when they are with you then that has to be better than a 'full-time' fractious mother. If you are weary and exhausted it is entirely appropriate for you to take steps to get the rest you need, so don't pile the guilt on top of the weariness.

FALSE GUILT

Guilt is the feeling that comes when we feel that we've not done as well as we'd like to have done, when we feel we have let ourselves down. The big question that needs answering is 'Am I really guilty?'. Here is the answer loud and clear:

When we make ourselves responsible for factors that were beyond our control the feeling that results is false guilt.
(If you are often beset with false guilt I'd advise you to write out and stick up that sentence in several prominent places around the home.)

If something goes wrong, or simply not as well as we'd like it to, the first emotion we feel is disappointment. There are degrees of disappointment. Maybe none of our kids inherited Mum's gorgeous red hair, or none of them have Grandpa's ear for music. These are disappointments about things we can't change. We can also feel disappointed with our children's behaviour. Perhaps they are just so unruly and stubborn or maybe they are so painfully shy. Maybe we're not disappointed by our kids but disappointed with ourselves about the things we cannot do for them, the toys we cannot afford to buy them, the people they miss such as Dad or a grandparent whom we cannot replace for whatever reason. Disappointment is a very painful and depressing emotion, but what's it got to do with guilt? *Guilt is the result when we take our disappointment in hand and go on a 'Who's to blame for this?' expedition.* We say things like 'My son is so aggressive because I'm so short-tempered with him' or 'my daughter's so clingy because I sent her to nursery far too early'. We try to account for our disappointment and we ask, 'Who is to blame for this situation?' and quite often our reply is, 'I am'. This is the point where disappointment turns into guilt. Sometimes on our blame-laying expeditions we find someone else to blame: 'These kids have never been the same since their father left us', or 'Their school friends have really led them away from me'. When this happens disappointment is transformed into anger, anger directed towards the person who we feel caused the disappointment. In effect we transfer the guilt on to them.

Disappointment can be a very intense and painful emotion but it is not destructive, it is just sad. When we deal with it by transforming it into self-destructive guilt or unforgiving anger, we give it the power to destroy us. We are allowed to feel disappointment about things that have not worked out for the best; we can truthfully acknowledge that our family break-up or our children's friends have had an negative influence. Disappointment about things we cannot change is legitimate (that means we are allowed to feel it). At the same time we have to acknowledge our part in the situation and we have to deal with any real guilt that we know we deserve in the constructive way that God has ordained: repentance. We must not destroy ourselves by holding ourselves on a guilty charge for factors we could not control. If we go back to the early years of parenthood the two factors that were most often beyond our control were inexperience and exhaustion. I'm not holding these up as excuses for deliberately harmful behaviour, but for most parents it is true that they can look back on their regrets and failures and say, 'Given the circumstances, we did our best, with the best motive'. Such parents do not have to hold themselves on a guilty charge simply because they were not 'perfect'.

Another example of a factor beyond our control is our work situation. Redundancy or relocation may have a devastating effect on our children, and if we could have prevented it we would have done so. Maybe you couldn't get your child into the school of your choice, or perhaps you simply didn't have the transport or finance to fund it. Perhaps a close friend moves away or a grandparent dies; both are situations that make us feel sad and disappointed but both are completely beyond our control. These situations come within the second area of parental experiences that leave us at the mercy of false guilt, and for the sake of simplicity I've defined all of these as 'If only' situations. We'll look at them in the next chapter.

Guilt can arise as a result of sin, but it also comes from the expectations society has of us and also from the expectations that we have of ourselves. False guilt is when we take responsibility for factors that were beyond our control. If we can rid ourselves from false guilt by deflating our sense of over-responsibility, we have only valid feelings of guilt left to contend with.

CHAPTER TEN

Guilt: 'If Only . . .'

'If only her best friend hadn't moved away.'

'If only he'd got into the other school.'

'If only we lived nearer to my parents.'

'If only . . . these things hadn't happened . . .' but they did and what's more you had no control over whether they happened or not, so the sense of guilt you feel is definitely false; disappointment would describe the feeling better. Sometimes, though, it is not always so clear whether our guilt is false or valid:

'If only I'd checked the temperature of the water before she'd got in.'

'If only I'd closed the stair gate behind me.'

'If only I'd checked the climbing-frame bolts.'

These are all factors that could have been in our control. These statements and the potentially dangerous accidents that lie behind them wrench a kind of agonised sympathy from other parents. It's a sort of self-protective sympathy. We rush out to check the climbing-frame bolts, having never thought of doing so before! Our hearts go out to the parents of children who have been maimed in accidents because we know we could so easily be in their place. We don't just feel for the suffering of the child, we feel acutely for the suffering of the parents. 'Accidents will happen' is hardly a comforting cliché when a loved and precious child is left disfigured. Nevertheless it contains a kernel of truth.

Accidents can and do happen to anyone and everyone, some of them with very tragic consequences. There is no malice or neglect behind most accidents since all it can take is a moment's inattention, and who of us could say 'hand on heart' that we have never been inattentive at any time? We all have equal potential for experiencing the kind of accident or trauma that leaves us with that awful longing to turn back the clock, 'If only . . .'.

Then there are those 'if only' situations where we feel we were definitely to blame, at least in part:

'If only his Dad and I were still together.'
'If only I'd bought him a cycle helmet.'
'If only I'd called the doctor sooner.'
'If only I'd checked who was collecting her from school.'

The list of potential accidents, mishaps and disasters that can happen to us is endless. No two situations are the same, so it would be impossible to lay down rules about who is to blame for what in every situation. Yet for an anguished parent the question 'Who is to blame?' is extremely important. They may well spend ages mulling over it. The result of their investigation could be that they either blame themselves 100 per cent and live the rest of their lives in the shadow of their 'failure', or they blame someone else and allow bitterness towards this third party to twist and spoil their whole outlook on life. Neither option takes away the misery of living with the result of the situation.

Blame-laying is, for the most part, a fruitless exercise. So how then do we come to terms with a situation for which we feel some degree of responsibility? There is a third option. Instead of blaming yourself or blaming others you could take your case to someone who knows all the facts and judges fairly. You could take your 'case' to the highest possible court, take it before God, the 'Judge of all the Earth'. 'Will not the Judge of all the earth do right?' said Abraham when he stood before God to plead a case (Genesis 18:25). This Judge knows you better than you know yourself, he 'searches' you and 'knows' you, he 'perceives your thoughts from afar', he is 'familiar with all your ways' (Psalm 139:1–4). Not only that, his word 'judges the thoughts and attitudes of the heart' (Hebrews 4:12). Surely here you are going to find out who was really to blame.

Picture yourself coming into his court. In your hands you are carrying the account of your 'case'. How are you going to plead? You may be trembling with remorse and plead guilty on all counts or you may be defending yourself in stammering tones. A big part of your whole dilemma is that you just don't know how much you are to blame. You steel yourself for the verdict but you are in for a surprise. He does not declare that you are guilty or innocent, instead he steps down from his throne, takes your notes from your hands and, ripping them up, declares joyfully, 'Case dismissed!' He flings his arms around you and says, 'I love you, let's leave all that stuff about blame behind and get on with life as it is now.' He doesn't do this because he's gone soft on sin; he does it when you are blaming yourself for factors you could not control. God is not in the business of apportioning blame but of forgiving sins. He does not keep a list of all your oversights and failings. If *we* insist on keeping such a list we will be severely hampered in our ability to love and care for our children now. False guilt leads us up an 'If only' alley. This is a one-way alley with a dead end. Listen to statements such as 'If only I'd not had them so close together', 'If only his Dad had been at his birth', 'If only he'd not had that accident'. None of these situations can be changed now. These 'If only' remarks are not only unproductive, they also stop us from asking the far more important 'What now?' questions. Whatever we regret in the past there is a more constructive response we can make if we would only ask 'What now?' instead of sighing 'If only'.

'Case Dismissed' is the best possible verdict for anyone going over and over an event trying to determine their level of guilt. But there is another verdict that God also loves to give and that is 'You're Forgiven'. These are the best possible words we can hear when we stand before God painfully aware of our shortcomings, failings and sins. When we've looked at all the factors, when we've interpreted the guilty signals, when we know for sure that we are totally deserving of our guilt, then the only way forward is repentance and making amends with whoever may have been hurt by our action.

All this makes repentance sound like a last ditch event: 'If all else fails we'll have to repent.' This is not the case; repentance should be a very regular, almost routine part of our lives because there are very many actions, words and attitudes in our lives which fail to honour God and which damage our relationships. I feel that we don't hear enough about repentance in the Christian community these days. We all know it is an essential first step when we become a Christian but after that it seems to get overlooked as we pursue more self-enhancing options such as exercising the gifts of the Spirit. Perhaps we have 'Christianised' the worldly goal of becoming a fulfilled person instead of demonstrating the goodness of God by acknowledging our own brokenness and dependency on him? No matter how mature and wise or gifted we become as Christians, at the heart of our faith we are and always will be a people who have had to be redeemed from our sins and who depend on God for his forgiveness.

WHAT IS REPENTANCE?

So what is repentance and how should we practise it? Put simply it is the confession of our sins to God together with a desire to change.

'If we confess our sins he is faithful and just and will forgive us our sins and cleanse us from all unrighteousness' (1 John 1:9).

This is the promise that God will pronounce a 'Not Guilty' verdict whenever we come to him. We are pronounced 'Not Guilty' even though we are guilty, because we are forgiven, and the punishment that we deserve was laid on Jesus. When he died 'he was pierced for our transgressions, he was crushed for our iniquities' (Isaiah 53:5). God's verdict is truly astounding so hear it said again if you need convincing,

'There is now no condemnation for those who are in Christ Jesus' (Romans 8:1). 'Come now, let us reason together,' says the Lord. 'Though your sins are like scarlet, they shall be as white as snow.' (Isaiah 1:18). 'In him . . . we have the forgiveness of sins, in accordance with the riches of God's grace' (Ephesians 1:7).

HOW SHOULD WE REPENT?

Some of you may feel you don't actually know how to repent, or perhaps you worry that you haven't done it 'right'. How should we repent? The answer is; specifically, frequently and thoroughly. Vaguely apologetic prayers of repentance spring from a vague sense of sin, and the antidote for this is to pray specifically 'Lord I'm sorry I spoke harshly to Anne', 'Lord, I'm sorry I've kept putting off going to see Karen'. Specific confession is more likely to lead to specific change, if only because you'll get fed up of confessing the same sin day after day. This brings us to the second point, repent frequently. Keep short accounts with God, at least daily. It's a great feeling to start each new day knowing you're forgiven for yesterday's mistakes. Finally, repent thoroughly. Often this means making amends perhaps by apologising to anyone hurt by your action or words.

I think the best advice about repentance is 'Just do it'. When we know that an honest and painful account of our own sins is required of us we suddenly become great procrastinators. We could also win awards for excuses. We might talk about God's love and his forgiving acceptance of us, just as we talk about the need to repent, but until we stop talking and 'just do it' we will not know the wonder of God's love and forgiving acceptance in our hearts.

PEOPLE WHO PUNISH THEMSELVES

There are two groups of people for whom repentance does not seem to work since they do not feel forgiven. The first group is made up of people who feel their sins are so awful and have had such terrible consequences in their lives or in the lives of other people that they cannot accept either a 'Case Dismissed' or a 'Not Guilty' verdict. They feel they deserve to be punished and if God won't punish them then they will punish themselves. They might say things like 'How can I ever forgive myself now my son's in a wheelchair' or 'I've destroyed my family because of adultery and I deserve my family's hatred and mistrust so I cannot accept forgiving love from either them or God'. If you think you cannot forgive yourself, the truth is not that you cannot but that you will not. What makes you think that your crime was so exceptional as to be excluded from any of the promises I've just quoted? Revelation 3:20 says, 'If anyone hears my voice and opens the door, I will come in and eat with him.' There is no exemption clause where you can insert your name. Your refusal to accept God's acceptance of you is itself a form of sin. It is an arrogant stubbornness that says 'I will atone (pay for) my own failures with my own misery'. The fact is your sin was atoned for by Jesus' sacrifice and he didn't do it in short measure, leaving us with a bit to do for ourselves; he atoned 'in accordance with the riches of God's grace' (Ephesians 1:7). If you feel you are to blame for some harm done to your child and none of these reasons persuades you to forgive yourself then ask yourself this question: 'What good does it do my child now for me to wrap myself up in my guilt?' It is simply not constructive.

THE PERFORMANCE TRAP

There is a second group of people for whom repentance never seems to work. These people never really feel 'forgiven' even though their sins are fairly minor. The reason they do not feel forgiven is because they are, often subconsciously, determined to impress God. No one can impress God, because 'all our righteous acts are like filthy rags' (Isaiah 64:6). We know it is true that we cannot impress God, but no end of us try. Have you never caught yourself thinking 'I'll talk to God about that later, I'm too irritated to talk to him now' or 'When I've had a better day, then I'll sit down and pray' or 'How on earth can I stop and worship God in the midst of all this stress in my life?' All of these thoughts reveal that we are holding God at a distance because we don't feel good enough. We rate our worth on our performance and only when we're performing well do we feel in touch with God. It is true that our sinfulness does form a barrier between us and God but it is a barrier we often try to dismantle or climb over by our own effort instead of coming straight to God in repentance and asking him to deal with it.

People who are bent on 'performance' think that they

have to feel 'spiritual' before they can come into God's presence, and the reality for most of us is that we do not feel spiritual very often. A hectic working day with cooking, ironing, fixing, fetching, shopping and sorting all added in, in short the rough and tumble of family life, does not lend any of us a pleasant aura of spirituality. We think 'If only we had some time to ourselves', or 'If only we were able to go on a retreat', then we'd feel close to God. Well, yes, you might and I don't want to undermine the value of quiet times or retreats but the reality is that you are close to God *now* in the hurly-burly of life. Whether you feel him or not, God is close to you.

We will not progress in our relationship with God until we come to him as we are and accept his acceptance of us at the very points and times when we feel unacceptable. Telling some people that God wants to share their daily life with them is like telling them the Queen is coming to tea. They are very happy to have her but 'For goodness sake, let me get the place tidied up first'. So they hoover the floor, rearrange the menu, plump up the cushions and arrange themselves into somehow looking spiritually presentable. Now God is royal, and it is not wrong to desire to please him, but this desire has to be born out of a knowledge that we cannot impress him. Not one of us is 'spiritually presentable'. We are all accepted as we are and are forgiven freely, we do not earn it by our performance.

So whether you've been beset by false guilt or hampered by deserved guilt there is a way forward. There is forgiveness. When you pour out your shame to him you can leave it for him to know how much of the guilt you don't deserve and as for the rest, the part you do deserve, he forgives you. If God forgives us but we cannot forgive ourselves, then our clinging on to guilt is a form of arrogance and stubbornness. We'd far rather do penance to make up for our failings than accept God's forgiveness as a free gift that we cannot possibly ever earn or deserve.

MAKING YOUR HOME A GUILT-FREE ZONE

Let's finish our discussion about guilt with three practical ways forward.

1) TAKE RESPONSIBILITY FOR WHAT IS NOW

Peter had made time one evening to sit down with the younger of his two daughters. Soon she would have to make important decisions about which subjects to continue with at school and these decisions would eventually determine her career choice. Peter felt he had a fairly good understanding of her abilities and interests, so after a while he tried to direct her towards a decision. Suddenly she becomes angry and uncooperative. When Peter asks her why she is suddenly annoyed she blurts out, 'You really wish I'd been a boy, don't you?' Peter is amazed by this outburst and even more taken aback by the memories she goes on to recall of conversations she'd overheard, conversations that had left her with the distinct impression that not having a son was a disappointment for him. For the life of him, Peter can't remember any such conversations but, dismayed by her visible hurt, he rakes over his attitudes and words to see if there is any truth in what she says. True enough, he'd often moaned at the whole family for their complete indifference to cricket, but as he adored both his girls how could she have got the impression that she was a disappointment?

Peter could now wrap himself up in guilt, a guilt he's not even sure he deserves. He could begin to blame his daughter's every insecurity on his supposed rejection of her. This in turn would make him insecure and defensive.

Instead of doing this Peter could listen to and accept his daughter's hurt feelings, accept her perception of the past. Without getting overly defensive he can apologise for unintentional hurt. He was not responsible for the way in which she has misinterpreted him, since it was a factor over which he had no control. Remember that in order to be rid of false guilt you must not make yourself responsible for factors you could not control. If he could not be responsible for changing misperceptions he didn't even know she had formed in the past, he can be responsible now these misperceptions have been expressed to do everything in his power to demonstrate to her that he does love her and is in no way disappointed with her.

If the cure for false guilt is to let go of the factors that were beyond our control then the cure for deserved guilt, once we've repented, is to take hold of the factors that are now within our control. Taking responsibility for the situation as it is now means refusing to waste time down 'If only' alley. Whether or not we caused the hurt, upset or accident there is no value in endless penance. Taking responsibility for what is now means planning new ways of listening, encouraging and reaching out to affirm, nurture and enrich our child.

Guilt sends us the message that says 'You've blown it, you've failed, it's too late now, you can't change'. Maybe for years you've given in to your aggressive teenager and feel too helpless to change your response now, and he is disappointed by your spinelessness and disrespects you. You just feel it's too late to change. God's accepting and forgiving love sends the message 'You can change, you can take responsibility for what is now'. If you feel a helpless failure don't give up and retreat, repent and press on. Repentance is owning responsibility for the part you had to play in whatever mess you face, but it is not wasting time with self-punishment or self-hatred. It is getting on with changing your way of behaving to take responsibility for what is now.

2) REPENTANCE AS A LIFESTYLE

If you allow the emotion of guilt to lie unattended in the background of your life it will become like a buzz of low-level interference. It will spoil your relationship with God and with your family and it will determine your behaviour. Even in the short term it warps our perspective of events and influences our decisions. For example, the other day before school my daughter was uncooperative. Later that same day I stood over her bed feeling guilty about how irritable and impatient I had been with her in the morning. This guilty message gnaws at me until the next morning when my daughter repeats her uncooperative behaviour. This time, drawing on all my resources of self-control, I respond with casual indulgence. I have rearranged my way of responding to the situation because of guilt. I am 'making up' for my impatience of the previous day. This goes some way to relieving my guilty feelings but at the end of the day she was still uncooperative and all she has learnt is that her mother behaves inconsistently! I have given her a mixed message because I allowed 'guilt' to be the controlling factor in determining my response. I would have been able to make a more consistent response if I'd got guilt out of the way first by repenting of my bad temper.

So we have to make repentance our lifestyle. Lifestyle is something that is seen, something that can be observed by others. When we make repentance a lifestyle it means that our spouses and children will see that repentance is a principle that operates in your life. It might not be appropriate for you to confess certain things to your family ('You're so ugly it annoys me' won't do a lot for your child's self-esteem!) but privately confessed sins such as 'I know I've shut the kids out of my life lately' or 'I'm sorry I'm always less tolerant of the older one' should have visible results. The process of change in your life should be obvious.

Sometimes you can be open about your failings. In our house it's common knowledge that Mum gets stressed out if we are late going somewhere. The fact that my anxiety is known and understood does not let me off the hook from handling it responsibly. Unfortunately our eldest child has inherited the same 'weakness'. This means the morning rush-hour in our house can be pretty explosive! My most frequent apology to the kids is the one I make as we walk to school. If I know I've messed up that morning by failing to pace myself I'll say something like, 'I'm sorry I got so harassed with you two this morning. You were ready by the door and I was in a flap'. Of course it's not always entirely my fault, so sometimes I say, 'Now how did we get on this morning? I know I really shouldn't have stopped to read the post but were there any other reasons we were late?' Often my openness to admit where I was wrong will give my children the space to admit that their attitude or action (grumpiness, lost shoes) was less than helpful. If I pin the blame entirely on them they become defensive, and defensive people rarely admit mistakes. Of course it wouldn't be good if I was constantly grovelling over my failures, it would give them room to manipulate me. The way you are open about your failures should increase your children's respect for you, not lower it. Our children need to see that as parents we are under God's authority and this authority means that we have to repent, obey and change. If they can see this principle at work in our lives it will make the authority we wield over them much more palatable. After all, why should we tell them what to do? Only because God tells us what to do.

3) REPENTANCE LEADS TO REAFFIRMATION

The message of God's forgiveness is that no matter how I have behaved I am loved and I am valued because of who I am, a chosen and loved child of God. By making repentance, forgiveness and reconciliation part of our daily lives we are trying to send this same message to our kids. We can sum the whole process up in one word: reaffirmation. We touched on this briefly in the second chapter on anger. Whenever we repent God reaffirms us. He says, 'I know you've messed it up but I forgive you and I still love you just as much. You are my child and I really believe that with my help you can do better next time.'

It's really important that we send the same message to our kids whenever they mess it up. If we have had to rebuke them, our reprimand should always finish with a reaffirmation of how much we love them and believe in them. This helps to remind both parent and child that it is the behaviour that is undesirable, not the person. Disciplining our children can often cause resentment on their side and guilt and uncertainty on our side. Practising reaffirmation until it becomes a normal part of our relationship will greatly reduce both our nagging guilt and their burning resentment. It cannot be helped that a confrontation or punishment will leave our children feeling a bit tender, so it's really important that we don't allow them to retreat licking their wounds without a reaffirmation to keep them company.

'You want them to feel bad about their behaviour not about the way you treated them as people.'[1] This piece of advice comes from Ken Blanchard, who wrote *The One Minute Manager*, a book advising managers about how to get the best out of their workforce. He recommends that after any reprimand you should take a deep breath, having shared your feelings about the way that this person's behaviour has affected you, then you should round it all up with a reaffirmation. For a parent this might be something like, 'You're a great kid and I really love you. I know you can do better.' It's sad that many managers might learn such useful principles in the workplace but fail to apply them at home.

The more aware we are of our own need for forgiveness the more we can extend that forgiveness to others. The command 'Be kind and compassionate to one another, forgiving one another just as in Christ God forgave you' (Ephesians 4:32) reminds us that we do not have an exclusive right to fouling up and starting over. We can and should allow our children that right. They must know that even if they really mess up they are still loved and precious to us. If God loves us, come what may, then surely our kids deserve no less. Isn't this the love that 'always protects, always trusts, always hopes, always perseveres'? (1 Corinthians 13:7).

Nor do we have an exclusive right to bad feelings. One of the most guilt-inducing experiences is not being able to 'fix' something for a disappointed child. Whether a child is sobbing over a broken toy or distressed because we cannot afford to send them skiing with the school, we should not deny them the right to these feelings just because they make us feel awful. We often resort to quick solutions or we try to 'jolly' them over things that are painful: a pet dying, a change of child-minder, a disloyal friend. Why do we do this? Because we cannot bear to see our children unhappy or in distress. Instead of facing the pain of that emotion with our child, we mistakenly try to protect them from bad feelings because we want them to be happy. But, they too have to own and face up to their negative feelings. When they are feeling bad, we need to face it, not fudge it.

In the end it is only who God is and what he has done for us that resolves our problems with guilt, false or deserved. He loves us, he knows us, he understands us, he forgives us, he gives us dignity and self-respect. 'This then is . . . how we set our hearts at rest in his presence whenever our hearts condemn us. For God is greater than our hearts and he knows everything' (1 John 3:19–20).

CHAPTER ELEVEN

Anxiety:
'You Can't Teach Children Anything'

Anxiety is . . . knowing your eight-year-old can swim ten lengths of the swimming pool but feeling uneasy when he wants to have a bath on his own.

Anxiety is . . . leaving your baby overnight with your Mum for the first time, telling her just what to do and when to do it, as if she'd never had a baby to look after before.

Anxiety is . . . your child's first day at school, leaving them in their over-large uniform with their lower lip trembling, their eyes appealing for you to stay with them.

Anxiety is . . . their first exam, their first game on the school team, their first boy-friend.

Anxiety is . . . an emotion woven into the fabric of parenthood. It is impossible to be a parent and not experience anxiety on a regular basis.

The focus of all we do as parents is to prepare our children for adult life. This huge responsibility consumes vast amounts of our time, money and effort. Not surprisingly, we worry from time to time whether we are getting it right. We don't simply want them to learn facts or skills such as how far is it to the moon or how do plants grow, we want to teach them concepts and values that are much broader and far more vital. Values such as honesty, consideration for other people, good use of time and self-discipline. Values that the media would have us believe are fast disappearing from the world in which our children are growing up. This leaves us with a scary sense of helplessness in the face of the rising tide of materialism, greed and self-centredness around us.

Even the older generation can seem unsympathetic. I recently overheard an elderly gentleman remarking on the younger generation, 'You can't seem to teach children anything these days.' 'What does he know about it?' I thought, feeling offended at first. However, the more I thought about what he'd said, the more I was inclined to agree with him. It *is* true. You cannot 'teach' children anything, in fact you never could 'teach' children anything, even in his day. All we have ever been able to do is give our children opportunities to learn for themselves and that is quite a different process.

I had an excellent science teacher at school. She was very strict but also made the lessons fun. She expected us to work out for ourselves the principle that lay behind whatever experiment we were conducting. It often took us a frustratingly long time to work out that A plus B plus heat equalled C, but we were much less inclined to forget the formula later. She made us feel as if we'd discovered it! I appreciate that not all teaching can be done this way; you can't really 'discover' a list of irregular verbs – you just have to learn them. However, when you apply this to parenthood I think the principle of 'letting them work it out for themselves' has a lot going for it.

Take 'sharing' as an example of a value we try to teach our children. 'It's so hard to teach them to share' is the most frequent remark made at our mother and toddler group, usually said as one small child is wrestling the Noddy car off another small child. Sharing is indeed a very difficult concept to 'teach' but all the mothers are instinctively going about it in the right way by bringing their children to the group, where they have an opportunity to learn that they are not the only little boy or girl in the world and that they do not have exclusive rights to the Noddy car. The mothers are not actually 'teaching' anything, all they are doing is creating an opportunity for the child to learn the art of sharing for himself. Even when you think you have successfully 'taught' a concept, you may find you've still got a long way to go. After a long lecture on sharing I gave a quartered peach to the elder of my squabbling children. She examined all the pieces closely and then handed the smaller, slightly bruised pieces to her brother. Catching my eye, she smiled sweetly and said, 'We're sharing, Mummy.' Sharing it may have been, but selfless altruism it certainly wasn't!

Then there is the matter of manners. How do you teach a child the words 'Please' and 'Thank-you' when his vocabulary consists of really useful words like 'Juice', 'More', or 'Mine'. You appeal to his self-interest and he learns that without the magic word the item he desires will not be forthcoming. Being well-mannered is simply a means to an end long before it is a desirable way to behave in its own right.

There are some concepts that are so big and hard to grasp that you cannot teach them to a child – you simply have to let the child experience them for himself. Time is a good example of this, because it is such a huge concept. When you have just turned three a third of your life lies between you and your next birthday! Tomorrow is a little out of focus and the end of the week is way over the horizon. On the penultimate day of her reception year I tried to prepare my daughter for the impending loss of her beloved reception teacher, 'Tomorrow is your last day at school', I told her. 'Really?' she said, looking at me, her eyes growing wide with amazement, 'My last day . . . ever?' I could see her thinking, 'Well, great, that's school over. Now can I be a train driver?' How could I break it to her that she actually had eleven more years to go? No amount of explaining could really enable her to understand.

Our children come into the world so vulnerable, so ill-equipped to cope with all that life will throw at them that watching them go out into the world on their own can tie us in knots of anxiety. Our instinct is to protect, nurture and guide our children, but part of that guidance is to allow them the freedom to make decisions and face consequences on their own. If our overbearing control never allows them to do this how will they learn? And yet allowing them that freedom is scary. We often want to step in and give them the benefit of our own lessons in life, and we hate to see them learn things the hard way. We instinctively want to protect our children from any hurt or stress even though we know that we ourselves have learnt as much from set-backs as from successes. We hate to see our kids make the same mistakes that we made. Take, for example the principle that 'if you don't revise you won't pass your exams'. How we'd love them to discover this principle before they fail! It is so hard to know how far we should go to protect our children. When they are very young we know what is best for them but it doesn't take them long to feel that *they* know what's best for them and from this moment on there is a constant tension over every choice we make.

The tension arises because our desire to guide and protect them has to be weighed up against their growing need and desire to assume ever greater responsibility for themselves. The responsibility devolved on us is awesome. Most of us can remember that feeling of amazement when we were allowed to come home from hospital with our first child – the feeling that we ought to have at least some qualifications for the task ahead. Some parents make up for their lack of qualifications by taking the whole business very seriously: they read all the books, take all the advice, buy all the safety gadgets, their children never have a sugary drink and eat raw vegetables. There's nothing wrong with any of this except when we substitute our tight control over our children's environment for a tranquil trust in our Father's active involvement in our children's lives. We have to learn to walk a fine line between making no effort at all to be a diligent parent and on the other hand becoming obsessively anxious about 'doing it right' and having our kids turn out okay. To quote again from *The One Minute Manager* by Ken Blanchard, 'If you manage only for profit it's like playing tennis with your eye on the scoreboard and not on the ball,'[1] Which, translated into the context of parenting reads, 'If you parent for success it's like playing tennis with your eye on the scoreboard not on the ball.' If you are constantly asking yourself 'how am I doing?' you will never enjoy the game.

Christian parents tend to veer to this side of the line. We tend to be 'hands on' type of parents, not 'hands off', because a certain degree of 'hands on' authority is our God-given responsibility. I do not want us to feel self-conscious about exercising appropriate authority, but I do think that we need to be wary of taking total control into our own hands. We need to get the balance right.

Our ultimate goal is that of working ourselves out of a job by turning out responsible, independent adults. If we over-protect and control, then the child cannot make the necessary small steps towards that goal. On the other hand if we give them too much responsibility too soon we risk them failing or being at risk. Whichever way you look at it, allowing our children to grow into independence is an extremely worrying process.

Trying to achieve the right balance is one of the main sources of anxiety as a parent. If you stop to think about almost any of the things that worry us about our children on a day to day level (apart from their health) you would find it boils down to this issue of protectiveness versus freedom. (Health is an example of a factor beyond our control, and I am going to consider the anxiety these factors cause us in the next chapter.) Another source of anxiety is also related to their growing independence: we feel anxious when we recognise that we are not going to be parents, in the sense we are now, for ever. We eventually have to reliquish our role as parents and if the role of parent has provided us with a sense of self-worth, security, a vocation or calling if you like, then the prospect of becoming 'redundant' can make us feel insecure and anxious.

Whichever way you turn, worry and anxiety keep cropping up as unavoidable facts of parenthood. How then can we keep our fears in perspective? Only by developing a *dependent trust* in the One who gave us our children and who wants to be with us as parents. Who can teach us the meaning of this *dependent trust*? Oddly enough the very people who we think have so much yet to learn: our children. Small children are often the best living demonstration of the attitude that we need to develop if we are going to cope with anxiety. Our offspring demonstrate *dependent trust* in us and we need to develop and demonstrate *dependent trust* in our Heavenly Parent.

BECOME LIKE A CHILD

When I was little I really believed that my Dad was a giant. He was six foot tall, well built with big, reassuring hands. I honestly believed that his arms could extend to reach anything I needed. He knew everything there was to know and could fix anything that needed fixing.

It's a delightful stage when our children feel that way about us. We might smile at their innocent awe and trust, but these qualities are very valuable. Sooner or later they will realise that we are not the supreme beings they once thought we were, but that doesn't have to undermine their trust. At some point I must have realised that my Dad's arms were not in fact extendable but I don't remember ever feeling disillusioned, because the awe and trust that had given rise to such a daft belief outlived the belief itself. Okay, so there were physical limits to the extent of his arms but there were no limits on the warmth of the welcome within them. So I had not trusted in vain. This attitude of dependent trust that we sometimes see in a small child is exactly the attitude we need to develop towards God, if we want to handle our natural anxiety. The one crucial difference of course is that our Heavenly Parent is the supreme being. He is worthy of our trust. He is all-knowing and infallible.

I am blessed with a three-year-old son who is very passive and obliging (most of the time!). As he accompanies me through each day, shopping, visiting friends, collecting his sister, I try to remember to tell him what we are doing and why we are doing it. But, because he is so easy-going, I sometimes forget to do this. As I strap him into the car for the third time that day or run him round to the neighbours at short notice, I am often struck by his unquestioning attitude and contented trust. If he thinks about it at all, he must think something like, 'I guess Mummy must know what she's doing or where she's going [if only he knew!] so I'll just tag along and fit in.' If only I had more of the same attitude towards God! Instead I question him constantly. I wonder what he's up to, doubting if he really has heard my concerns, worrying whether he really has my highest good in mind even though he's promised me he has (Romans 8:28).

Dependent trust is a difficult attitude to develop, firstly because deep down we wonder if God is really trustworthy and secondly because we are so fiercely independent. We like to feel in control of our lives.

SELF-RELIANCE RULES?

Society screams independence at us; 'Be your own man', 'Make your own choices', 'Take charge of your own life', these are all messages the advertisers use to enhance their products, because independence appeals to us. Independence is seen to be a valuable, even essential, personal quality. The emphasis on being fulfilled, in control of your life, independent and free from outside authority stems from the belief that to depend on anyone else is to be weak. If you were to canvas opinion about what would be the ten most important abilities for a parent to have, people might mention the ability to budget, the ability to drive, the ability to be organised, the ability to be patient and calm. I suspect that very few would mention the ability to trust someone else for the things you cannot do. And yet God considers this ability essential for successful living and asks us to depend on him: 'Trust in the Lord with all your heart and lean not on your own understanding; in all your ways acknowledge him, and he will make your paths straight' (Proverbs 3:5,6). John 15:5 puts it even more bluntly: 'I am the vine; you are the branches. If a man remains in me and I in him, he will bear much fruit; *apart from me you can do nothing*' (emphasis mine).

In contrast to this statement parents today are expected to do everything and often alone, without the help of the wider family since even if grandparents or aunts live nearby, they too are being urged by society to live their own lives and not be hampered with someone else's problem. Independence has led many to isolation. It's hard enough for many people to rely on anyone else and even harder for them to rely on God.

Last year God taught me about my own independent attitude. Through the things I was reading and through a series of circumstances he pointed out that although I had no problems helping other people, when it came to them helping me, I felt decidedly uncomfortable. My feeling of self-worth rested largely on my own sense of competence and if I had to ask for help then my sense of self-worth was undermined. One night in a Bible study group the words of a song had particularly spoken to me,

> Brother, let me be your servant,
> Let me be as Christ to you,
> Pray that I might have the grace to
> Let you be my servant too.[2]

Not long after this I came down with a heavy cold. I still had to do my weekly shop so I was dosing myself up and preparing to go ahead anyway. Just as we were about to leave my neighbour arrived at my door. A good friend and a lively Christian, it was usually a joy to see her but this time her opening words flattened me,

'You look dreadful,' she said.

'Thanks a lot,' I thought instantly feeling ten times worse, but before I could even muster up a weak smile she followed up with, 'Anyway, don't worry, because I've had it from God I'm meant to do your shopping today, so here I am, give me your list.'

I was very taken aback. I'd never heard her so forthright before. She is usually very mild-mannered and not given to issuing edicts from the Almighty. I blustered for two or three minutes, trying to think of every reason under the sun as to why she should not do my shopping, 'There's too much to do', 'It'll take too long'. . . . Eventually it became clear that she wasn't going to budge so, with the words of the song above ringing in my head, I handed over the list.

As I closed the door behind her I knew my bluster had been false. The real reason why I didn't want her to do my shopping was because I didn't think she'd do it properly. I took a great deal of pride in the way I did the shopping. Living on a tight budget means strictly one big shop a week, buying everything you need in one go and thus not risking an expensive return trip to the store. I thought she'd forget things and buy the wrong brands. So I was very annoyed at her (and God's) insistence that she do my shopping. 'I'm sure this will just make extra work, Lord,' I reasoned. 'You know I'm good at it, why couldn't you let me do it?'

Far from being ashamed at such an ungrateful attitude, a feeling of annoyance settled over me. As there didn't seem any point in staying in with two children and a bad mood I decided to take the kids to the park for half an hour. They ran off joyfully towards the swings and slides when we arrived and I sat down on the bench, trying to make the most of the rest. After a few minutes both children wanted to go on the swings. We went over to the baby swings and my younger child immediately reached up his arms, all keen and eager for his go on the swing, happy to accept my help to lift him into the chair. I offered the same help to my daughter who was, at five years old, still too small to climb into the bucket style seats by herself. Or at least that's what I thought. I received a curt rejection, accompanied by a fierce 'I'll do it by myself'. I know all about the value of the 'Do it by myself' stage so I stood back and watched as she struggled for a full five minutes to get into that swing seat. She did eventually succeed but had lost five minutes of happy swinging time. Five minutes which her brother had enjoyed to the full. As I watched the one struggling and the one swinging I felt God saying, 'Which one are you most like? I send help for you but you'd prefer to struggle on alone. You don't want to depend on me and you turn your back and prefer to do things by yourself.'

I had to admit he was right. I came to see that there is no value in the kind of independence that has to be maintained at all costs because it is a statement of my competence and control. If my value and self-worth lies in who God declares me to be, a loved and forgiven child, then it cannot be undermined by my 'failure' to be competent and capable. On the other hand if I perceive my value as being based on my competence then I must be competent at all times or else my self-image will crumble completely.

By the time I'd got back from the park I'd done some serious repenting and was able to be sincerely grateful to my neighbour for her help. This, in spite of the fact that I did have to go back to the store again later! I was grateful for the far more important lesson that God had brought home to me that day – dependence on him or on others did not undermine my value or worth in his sight.

In the secular world self-esteem is based on being pleased with who we are. For Christians the basis for healthy self-esteem is being pleased with who God says we are. He wants us to rejoice in who we are: children of God, loved, individually created and gifted. It is not healthy to be painfully self-conscious or destructively negative about ourselves. God does not ask us to have a worm-like mentality. At the same time he doesn't want us to forget that we are who we are because he chose us, 'But God chose the foolish things of the world to shame the wise' (1 Corinthians 1:27). We do what we do because he enables us, 'Not that we are competent in ourselves to claim anything for ourselves, but our competence comes from God' (2 Corinthians 3:5). 'But we have this treasure in jars of clay to show that this all-surpassing power is from God and not from us' (2 Corinthians 4:7). Even our weaknesses are an opportunity for his strength to be revealed: 'My grace is sufficient for you, for my power is made perfect in weakness' (2 Corinthians 12:9).

It might sound like I'm stating the obvious to say that as Christians we are not meant to be independent, self-governing people; we are meant to be dependent, obedient people. When it is put as bluntly as that I expect you'd have no problem agreeing with me. The problem comes in the nitty-gritty of daily life when we revert to independent self-government instead of dependent trust.

HOW CAN WE MAINTAIN AN ATTITUDE OF DEPENDENT TRUST?

1) It helps to remember that our trust is not placed in a formula but in a person. When we trust in a person we rely on who he is. If my husband leaves a message to say he'll be late home from work but gives no reason, I believe that he has been unavoidably delayed and I trust that it is not because he doesn't feel like coming home or has found something more appealing to do. My trust ultimately rests on the promises he made on our wedding day. It has been built up and strengthened by my experience of his faithfulness during the years of our marriage.

God is a person we can trust in exactly the same way. He has given us solemn promises about his care and love for us and the longer we have known him the more we can look back and see how he's been faithful to those promises. Strengthened by his promises which have been reinforced by our experience, we can keep our fear and anxiety about today and the future in perspective. We trust him for who he is, not because he gives us all the answers. Joni Eareckson Tada wrote, 'Lord I don't expect to survive because you roll out in front of me the blueprint behind my painful experiences. I don't live on reasons why. I live on your promises.'[3] Here is someone expressing that attitude of dependent trust, the attitude that says, 'I may not know what God is doing but I trust him because I know who he is and I know he's on my side.'

I have a fridge magnet that sums up the same attitude. It is of two little bears looking up at the big Daddy bear.

Their large brown eyes are round with an unspoken question. The big bear is raising his paws as if to give the final word on the matter. All he says is, 'Because I'm the Daddy, that's why.'

How often do we hear ourselves saying a similar thing to our children: 'Because I say so, that's why.' We ask them to trust us and we require their obedience even if they disagree or do not fully understand our reasons. If we expect our children to trust us then we should be demonstrating a similar trust in our Heavenly Parent.

2) We need to keep short accounts of our fearful feelings. Don't allow a worry to go on and on without placing it, regularly, in God's hands. We need to be seen to be putting our fears and concerns into God's hands. We need to be honest about the worrying things we cannot control and obviously leave these worries with God (provision for our needs, safety when travelling, health). We need to relax our grip on the things we think we can control (our children's friendships, their success in exams) and trust God to protect them in the times and places when they are beyond our protection.

TRAVELLING COMPANIONS

We are on a journey with our children and year by year we release to our children more and more responsibility to do the things they are capable of doing at whatever age they are at (spending their own pocket money, feeding a pet, running an errand alone). Progress on this journey is made by the parents slowly letting go one by one all of the things they were responsible for at the beginning. Ulrich Schaeffer has written the following prayer and it sums up so well just how nerve-racking this journey can be.

Lord,
sometimes I am frightened by the weight I feel
to bring up these children
that you have entrusted to me
because in our time,
full of confusion and potential,
it seems harder and harder
to know how to raise children.

I know I will make mistakes,
that I will fail my children,
that my strength and patience will not be sufficient,
that I will make the wrong decisions,
and that at times my love will grow weak.

Around me I see parents
labouring under the same weight,
afraid in the same way,
trying their best,
reading, feeling, growing
to stay close to their children
so that they will have the best possible start.

Help us all to keep love going,
and to put your blessing on our love
which then has a chance to overcome
all the mistakes we will make.
Help us to know what it means practically
to be real companions to our children.[4]

In what sense, I wonder, are we companions to our
children? Surely in the sense that we are all on a journey,
learning how to trust and depend on God more and more
deeply. When our children are young we ask them to
trust us. We try to be trustworthy, we try to be a reliable
reflection of the trustworthiness of God. But we know all

too well how unreliable we are and how much we ourselves need to trust God for the times when we fail or when we make mistakes. We hope and pray that one day they will transfer their trust in us to a trust in the same Heavenly Parent whom we have trusted throughout the journey. Dependent trust in our Heavenly guide is an attitude we must develop if we are going to enjoy the journey. It is an attitude that will see us through the day to day humdrum of being a parent. At some time or another on our journey a crisis or anxiety will arise, so large that our fear overwhelms us and it will feel like our Heavenly Guide has left us and we may well wonder, 'Should we have trusted him after all?'

CHAPTER TWELVE

Anxiety: 'Can I Really Trust God to Look After My Kids?'

The phone rings in the middle of the afternoon. It's the school secretary. Before she finishes her first sentence your heart is pounding. As you put down the phone only a few of her phrases are ringing in your head, 'An accident . . . your son . . . go to Casualty'. You are thinking and moving around very quickly and yet at the same time everything seems to be in slow motion. You dither over the cooker, should you turn the oven off? Will he still want his tea? Will he be home for tea? As dreadful possibilities pile in on you from every direction you attempt to pull yourself together. Perhaps it'll just be some minor injury . . . a few stitches . . . but then again . . .?

These sorts of sudden crises are the stuff of our worst nightmares. They induce worry in panic proportions and are, thankfully, short-lived and infrequent. Sometimes, though, a crisis will develop into a long-term problem: an accidental injury requiring lengthy treatment or maybe a one-off warning from the police leading to long-term worry about the company your teenager keeps. Or maybe a persistent minor illness that besets a child – will she ever be rid of it? Could it be an indication of a worse condition?

Anxiety is not usually a sudden and short-lived emotion. It is a feeling that we live with day in, day out. Stop for a moment and think of a problem you are worrying about right now. Thought of something? Right, picture that worry in your mind as an island in the middle of an ocean. You are on that island and worry is like the well-worn coastal path around that island. You are going round and round, regularly reaching 'Crisis Point', but never actually finding a way off. You look out over the Sea of Circumstances surrounding your island but it is too choppy to risk any bold attempt to escape from the problem, so you turn and go back to the well-worn worry path and trudge round and round. How can you ever be rescued from your island, from this problem? What you need is someone else to notice, understand your distress and come to your aid. You need an 'air-lift'. At the risk of sounding corny I could say a 'prayer lift' but the trouble with persistent worriers is that not only do they worry about their problem, they also worry about the quality of the rescue service! So the very idea of prayer at a time like this raises all sorts of its own worries: what if God doesn't notice our distress flares? What if he doesn't get here in time? Even if he does turn up, will he do want I want him to do? Does he really have the power to do anything anyway?

'Give it to God in prayer' can sound like an astonishingly simplistic and insensitive suggestion to make to someone who is wrecked with worry and fear. The first thing that must be given to anyone in distress or anxiety is permission to feel whatever they are feeling: anger, confusion, fear, guilt. The whole range of negative emotions is valid, and asking or expecting people to piously put their feelings to one side is extremely unhelpful. Jesus sanctioned the display of strong emotions by weeping at Lazarus' tomb and being angry in the temple, and if we need further evidence that emotions are okay we can look in the Psalms. Maintaining emotional neutrality is not a mark of spiritual maturity. Just as the emotions of distressed parents are valid, so are their questions. Can God really handle this problem? Will he come through for them? Does he really care about them and their kids? This chapter is going to try to deal with some of these questions by boiling them down to the one big question: 'Can I really trust God to look after my kids?'

THE BIG QUESTION

In the last chapter we saw how developing an attitude of dependent trust would help us keep our day to day worries in perspective. By trusting in God for who he is and by keeping short accounts with our fearful feelings, we are less likely to be overwhelmed by anxiety. The trouble is, although we need to practise this attitude of dependent trust at all times, most of us only try it out when we are desperate. So, having not given much thought to God's protection and care while things are running along smoothly, when something goes badly wrong the question 'Where is God in all this?' becomes a very big question indeed.

It's a question we need to have answered during the good times, when we feel blessed, when we sense his presence and protection. It's a case of not forgetting in the dark what God told you in the daylight. In the dark and desperate times when we cannot feel God or understand what he's doing, we have to hang on to our knowledge of what he is like and our previous experience of him. Moments of doubt and desperation will surely come to us all, and when they do the biggest temptation is to feel that God has changed and that suddenly he loves us less, that he is less committed to us. This is not true – God does not change. He is as loving in the daylight as he is in the dark. Whether we feel it or not he loves us, cherishes us and feels for us in our pain. We don't need to add guilt to our list of negative feelings when something goes wrong – the guilt of not feeling God's love for us. If our emotions are stretched to their limit experiencing pain, anger or anxiety, it's hardly very surprising that they have difficulty registering peace and love. If we *do* feel positive in the face of a crisis, it is the work of God's Spirit and not any credit to us. What matters is that no matter whether we feel God's love or not, we have to hang on to the fact of God's love. Believing in this fact is a bit like wearing a life-jacket when you've been thrown overboard on a dark stormy night. The life-jacket doesn't protect you from feeling the cold or from feeling afraid but it does keep your head above water . . . just! So then, the more we know and practise what it means to have dependent trust in a loving God over our minor worries, the better we will be able to hang on when we are thrown overboard by events and our pain blots out everything else.

WHO'S IN CHARGE AROUND HERE?

It seems to me that the question 'Can I really trust God to look after my kids?' arises when we haggle with God over the question of responsibility. Who is responsible for keeping our kids safe? Is it me? Or is it you, God? Just who is in charge around here?

The answer to this question is not as simple as you might at first think, so let's put it in the form of a picture. I'd like you to imagine that you are a gardener. You have been given a little garden, full of beauty and potential. It is your job to nurture, develop and protect this garden. Unfortunately your little garden is placed in the middle of a jungle and from this jungle all sorts of wild creatures and unsavoury weeds threaten to invade and spoil your garden. So what do you do? You build a fence around your little garden to keep it safe. At first this seems easy as the outside dangers are easily identified and eliminated and you are in control of the situation. However, as your garden grows it seems that gaps appear in your fence and all sorts of interactions are going on between your garden and the jungle, and things are running out of control.

Now let's apply this parable to parenthood. We are each gardeners, our children are our garden and the jungle is the world. From the first moments when we take our new-born infant in our arms, our natural desire is to nourish, protect and cherish this child. This is relatively easy at first; warmth, love and food are about all he needs. Sure it can be hard work providing these but usually we're capable. As our baby grows we buy stair-gates, lock away disinfectants and invest in cycle-helmets, and so we should – not to do so would be negligent. It *is* right and appropriate for us to build that protective fence. The danger comes when we trust more in our own safety measures than in the all-powerful and all-loving protection of God. Before we know where we are we have placed our complete confidence for our child's safety and well-being in our own hands instead of God's.

We know that we should be responsible, careful parents but we should not delude ourselves into thinking that we are capable of building a fence of protection big enough or strong enough to keep our child safe at all times. From the moment your child takes his first step, through every milestone, God invites you on a tour of 'fence inspection' with the sole purpose of pointing out the gaps in your fence and calling for you to trust him to fill these gaps. Their first disappointment in friendship, their first time away from home overnight, their first date. All of these potentially nerve-racking situations ought to unravel our reliance on ourselves and deepen our dependence upon God. Each small step of faith is somehow a rehearsal or reminder of the larger truth that our children are ultimately in God's care. As our children get older we have to increasingly acknowledge that we cannot always be on hand to help them out, nor can we always be there for them. Our feelings of love and protectiveness don't diminish as our children grow in independence and the gaps in the fence get wider. Trusting God for these gaps is the only way to live with our anxiety for our children without becoming over-protective.

In fact the gaps in the fence were there from the start. We have never been fully in control. For example, we have never had the power to protect our children from disease and illness, nor could we control our children's genetic inheritance. These are factors totally beyond our control: our daughter may carry a faulty gene that will bring heart-ache and havoc in her life, and we cannot influence this situation. Less seriously, we cannot even dictate the type of personality our child will have: will she be affectionate, compliant and passive or will she be determined, committed and inflexible? The more willing we are to acknowledge just how much is beyond our control, the more likely we are to depend more deeply on the God who created and gave us our child. The problem comes when we say to ourselves, 'Well, if I am not in control and God *is* in control then why do things go wrong? Is he really in control?'

AND THE FACTS ARE . . .

The Bible teaches us two facts about God and our kids. They are facts that we tend to pass over rather glibly:

1) God created our children. 'For you created my inmost being; you knit me together in my mother's womb' (Psalm 139:13).

2) God gave us our children as a gift. 'Sons are a heritage from the Lord, children a reward from him' (Psalm 127:3).

If you stop to take in these facts then their implications can change the way you think. The first reminds us that God is the giver of life. We cannot dictate when life begins or ends, God reserves this right and knowledge: 'All the days ordained for me were written in your book before one of them came to be' (Psalm 139:16). Whether a created life lasts 72 days or 72 years we are to make the most of each day that it is given and not take it for granted. This brings us to the second fact which reminds us that children are a gift. You cannot control a gift, you cannot dictate when it will arrive or what it will be like, you can only receive it. These two facts are motivating and important truths for all parents. For parents who have received and cherished children who are in any way handicapped or children whose lives were painful and brief these truths can become a ballast against a tide of despair.

God would like us all to know that not only did he create our children and 'gift' them to us, he is the one who can protect them, guide them, and sustain them. We like to see this as being our job and, whilst it is true that God has devolved responsibility on to us to care for our children, we must not think that he has wandered off and left us to get on with the job.

GOD DOES NOT SELL INSURANCE

What most of us would like to know is: 'If I trust God will life be smooth and accident-free and will my kids be safe and happy?' Is trusting in God the same as taking out an insurance policy against accidents, disasters and disease? Parenthood offers such scope for these crises that if God did offer any such insurance policy he would surely be a lot more popular than he appears to be. Trusting in God, however, is not about avoiding crises but about knowing God is right there with you through all of life's events.

Children will play hairdressers with the kitchen scissors, they will explore sockets with knitting needles, they are likely to wander off in crowded places, the list of potential traumas is endless. How much we'd like to be spared tragic and painful experiences.

Trusting in God is not a way of calling down some divine blanket ban on unpleasant experiences but it is a way of knowing that God is with us, can strengthen and sustain us through everything. Everything from the trivial and mundane to the tragic and painful. It is a fact that we live in a fallen world, a world that is not running the way God intended it to run, a world that has turned its back on its creator. This results in corrupt people, disasters, disease and death. We cannot avoid the effects of living in a fallen world any more that we could avoid breathing in polluted air in an inner-city traffic jam. It is not our fault, but our children will get sick, they will be involved in accidents and they will be hurt by other people be it accidentally or maliciously. Maybe something sad has already happened to you or to your child and this has severely weakened your trust in God. Where was God when you needed him? Why didn't he cure your child's cancer? Why did your daughter fall in with that crowd and end up in such trouble? Why did God allow this? How we'd love some neat spiritual insurance policy that would guarantee our children's safety. These traumas cause us so much pain, yet when we come banging on heaven's door for an answer it can often seem like no one is there. Has God abdicated his responsibility? Has he let us down? It can feel that way.

You should never be afraid to have a good shout and rant about your pain. It is right and helpful to acknowledge just how bad we feel. David could say, 'You are God my stronghold. Why have you rejected me?' (Psalm 43:2). God will not fall off his throne in surprise, nor will he go off in a huff. But when all is said and done God did not let you down, nor is he distant, most often it is the noise of your own pain that prevents you from hearing the weeping of a God who never intended his children to suffer such heartache and pain and who did not inflict this on you wilfully or malignantly.

In spite of his power and ability and trustworthiness he did not offer any of us an insurance policy against the effects of living in a fallen world, nor will he turn us into robots by removing personal responsibility and choice from us, nor can he spare us the painful consequences of wrong choices.

SO WHY TRUST?

So why trust in a God who appears to do so little? It's a rather brief answer to a very big question, which has been better dealt with by others[1] but God has promised that come what may he will not abandon us and he will bring us through whatever life throws at us if we throw ourselves on him in trust. It is right for us to pray for protection and for healing, and he does graciously answer these prayers more times than we are aware or grateful for. However, we cannot demand that he answer us in the way we require. He is God Almighty, not some cosmic computer that will turn events around to suit us if only we know how to key in the right command. His highest desire for us is not that we would live a life free of suffering and pain but that all of life's experiences will deepen our knowledge and trust in him. He has promised that he will bring us ultimately to a place without tears, where sorrow and heartache have no place.

Trust that is based on total knowledge of the situation can hardly be called trust. Like our own children who have to trust us when they can't understand what's going on, we too are called to trust that God cares for us even when things are not going the way we'd like. Even though God has given us many wonderful promises about his love and his power, we cannot 'control' God by quoting these at him. This truth was wonderfully illustrated for me when my little lad started playgroup. He found the idea of being left in a strange place full of noisy children quite unpalatable. It didn't do any good to tell him about the sand-pit or the train set, the Lego or the playdough; as far as he was concerned the only good thing about playgroup was coming home at the end! As it seemed unrealistic to expect him to 'enjoy' it at first I turned my attention to reassuring him that he would survive it. I found out that the session always ended with a group story-time, so I promised him that 'Mummy would come back after the story'. This reassured him on two counts. It told him I would come back and when I would come back, 11.45 am being a bit meaningless to a three-year-old. So leading up to his first day, we repeated this promise like a mantra, 'So you'll come back after the story?' 'Yes, I'll come back after the story.' On his first day I left him making a noble attempt to be very brave, mouthing the words of the well-worn promise through the window at him as I left. He nodded solemnly. What happened next was recounted to me by the playgroup leader when I duly returned at the appointed time. Matthew had made the best of the situation for about half an hour and had then decided he'd had enough and 'could he please go home now?' Faithful to the formula I'd given him he trotted over to the book corner, selected a story and put himself on the knee of an unsuspecting helper. Quite naturally, she read him the story. When they reached the end he looked round expectantly and then burst into tears. 'Mummy said she'd come back after the story,' he managed to blurt out between heart-rending sobs. He had not been able to make Mummy magically reappear and it had taken the helpers a good twenty minutes to calm him down.

It can often feel that God lets us down in the same way that I let Matthew down that day. He fails to come through for us in the way we'd like. This doesn't alter the stated facts of his love for us. He could make no greater statement of love than he has already made by giving up his Son for us. In order to put our fear and anxiety to one side, in order to be rid of the bitterness and resentment we have held on to, we have to repent for our lack of trust in God's demonstrated and stated care for us. Lessons in trust are never popular. Thankfully the larger part of our experience as parents is filled with the more trivial and mundane type of disasters: ear infections, scraped knees, crooked teeth and mild acne. I'm not suggesting these things are not painful and upsetting. Let's not underestimate their effect, but they are the stuff of an ordinary childhood, as are such normal crises as moving house, a pet dying, or getting a bad school report. All of these are opportunities to develop and practise dependent trust in a God whose presence is, by itself, the greatest comfort. At a time of particular stress and anxiety I was given a hand-written motto that remained permanently on the mantelpiece: 'Peace is not the absence of trouble, it is the Presence of God.' How do we nurture such an awareness of God?

CHAPTER THIRTEEN

Be Nurtured Yourself

There are some days when I feel like I am a 'clockwork Mummy'. I get up, I get the children off to school, I work, I fetch the shopping, I pay some bills, then it's time to collect the children. I ferry them to their next activity. I do some chores. I pick the children up again. I cook tea, we put the children to bed and then . . . the clockwork unwinds; and I collapse exhausted into the nearest armchair. Then the whole routine starts again the next morning. I wonder if you've ever felt like that?

When your days are dictated by either the school timetable, your work deadlines or your bank statements, it can feel like you are no longer in charge. You are just a necessary cog that needs to turn through the motions in order to keep family life going: the beds must be made, the bills must be paid and work must get done.

On better days my collapse into the armchair will be timed to coincide with a cup of tea made for me by my husband. He knows from experience that five minutes spent clutching a warm mug of 'amber nectar' and staring vacantly into space through its steam, will do much to revive me. It's at this time of the day, having helped put our own kids to bed, that I day-dream about what it would be like to be a child again and be 'put to bed' myself. How restful it would be to have someone say they've run a hot bath for me, they've warmed my pyjamas on the radiator, they're happy to read me *three* stories if I'd like and then they'll kiss me on the forehead and say 'Night, Night, Sleep tight'. They'll leave the door ajar and I'll drift off to sleep comforted by the low light from the landing and the hum of adult conversation downstairs.

Just thinking about it unwinds me!

Much of this book has focused on the stresses and demands that we face in our lives as parents, but we started out with the idea that only by having a relationship with God as our perfect parent can we be strengthened to withstand the pressure our own parenthood puts on us. I'd like to return to this theme in this last chapter because if I leave you now with only practical advice ringing in your ears you might fall into the trap of thinking that there is a neat formula for handling life as a parent. For all that I've said, the key to being a better parent does not lie in greater effort, greater self-awareness, assertiveness training, active listening or in any other strategy that I may or may not have mentioned. The real 'hope for the hard-pressed parent' lies, not in a method or discipline, but in vital relationships and in one vital relationship above all others, the relationship between you and God. This is the key (if something so indefinable as a relationship can be called a key) to the art of imperfect parenting.

VITAL RELATIONSHIPS

One can only nurture and be nurtured in the context of relationships. The dictionary defines to 'nurture' as to care, to nourish, sustain and train. It is well known that children cannot simply be fed and watered: they need to be loved in order to thrive. Nor can they receive love in a one-off dose. Nurture is an ongoing experience. It cannot be done in a moment, because a relationship is a growing, changing thing. Just as the nurture of our children is a continuously changing process, so the relationships we have with those who nurture us must be growing and deepening. Being nurtured ourselves will go a long way towards helping us nurture our children. Relationships that nurture us can be said to be vital.

If we all sat down and wrote a list of the vital relationships in our lives we would all have a different list. Not just different people, of course, but different types of people. We may or may not have a spouse, some of us may have close family who figure greatly in our lives, others will have more vital relationships with friends. However our list is made up, we all need a certain number of these relationships. We need people who care for us, who encourage us, who make us laugh, who are willing to pray with us, who will disagree with us. We might not find any one person able to do all of these things so we need a small circle of faithful friends with whom we can be ourselves. A faithful friend is not necessarily someone who is in the same position as you are. For example, although friendships with other parents are a great source of sympathy and understanding most fellow parents are under the same pressure as we are, so their resources of time and energy are as limited as ours. Friendships with people at a different stage of life can be a refreshing reminder that not everyone sees the world as we do. The most essential qualification for a friend is not that they are like you, nor that they are at the same stage of life as you, nor that they agree with you, but that they are 100 per cent on your side. That doesn't mean they have to overlook your faults; they might challenge you or confront you, they may even criticise you, but if they have shown by their words and deeds that they are fundamentally committed to your well-being then their friendship is of great value to you.

The Bible clearly teaches that the husband-wife relationship is meant to be a vital relationship, rich in mutual affirmation and support. The Bible is also realistic enough to point out that such a relationship doesn't happen automatically but has to be worked at. We have to commit ourselves to the task of knowing and loving our spouses. Once we have children this task can get a lot harder. It is not uncommon for weary parents to pass like strangers on the dark landing between their offspring's bedroom and their own. Simple things like talking and listening to each other will not happen unless we plan for it and hold each other to that plan. You may not be able to afford one night out a week but there is no reason why you should not have one night 'in', preferably with the telly switched off and with the phone disconnected. Talking, sharing and understanding will not happen unless you provide the right atmosphere.

Apart from your spouse, the next most important relationship in your life might be one or two people with whom you can pray. Combining three people's diaries is harder work than combining two, so I have always found having a prayer partner more helpful than having a prayer triplet. But there is something to be said for either way of getting together to pray. The important thing is not how you pray but *that* you pray. There are few things more helpful than someone to whom you can make yourself accountable on a weekly basis and they to you. Someone with whom you can talk through dilemmas and pray over possibilities.

Finally you need people to have fun with. Hopefully your spouse and prayer partner are not excluded from the 'fun people to be with' category! You need people to exercise with, go to the cinema with, eat with and generally enjoy life with. Life is full of people and things that demand our attention urgently and it is all too easy for the urgent to squeeze out the important. Friends are important so we need to ensure that time with them is not squeezed out of our schedules.

ONE VITAL RELATIONSHIP

At certain times of your life you may have a very long list of people with whom you have the kind of vital relationships that I've just described. There will be other times when your list will seem very thin. Whether you have many friends or few, there is one vital relationship which you cannot live without. This is because this relationship is the source of life itself. The psalmist wrote, 'For with you is the fountain of life' (Psalm 36:9). Jesus called himself 'the bread of life' (John 6:35), and said that he came for men to have 'life and life in all its fullness'. But is our definition of 'life in all its fullness' the same as God's definition? Did Jesus come so that I might have a smooth, comfortable, trouble-free existence? Did he come to make me feel fulfilled, successful and affirmed? No, he didn't. He came that I might know God. That I should have a relationship with God is God's primary purpose for me. Whatever else happens in my life is of secondary importance.

God's definition of 'life in all its fullness' is a relationship with him through his Son. 'And this is the testimony: God has given us eternal life, and this life is in his Son. He who has the Son of God has life; he who does not have the Son of God does not have life' (1 John 5:11, 12).

Jesus rebuked those who thought that life could be defined and attained by adherence to some religious formula: 'You diligently study the Scriptures because you think that by them you possess eternal life. These are the very Scriptures that testify about me, yet you refuse to come to me to have life' (John 5:39, 40). Thus he confirms that 'to have life' is defined as having a relationship with him. God is more committed to having this relationship with us than we are with him. We are more committed to our well-being, none the less he relentlessly pursues his goal for us to know him and trust him more deeply through every situation of our lives. We would prefer to arrange life in a way that would maximise our personal comfort and sense of fulfilment but God's priority, in every situation, is that we are drawn closer to him. Thus disappointments, hurts, pressure, hard work, difficult relationships, all such unpleasant situations, can be opportunities to deepen our dependency on God. He is not indifferent to the pain these situations cause us and he does not inflict them on us maliciously. They happen to all the inhabitants of this fallen world but when they happen to us the highest good that can come from them is that our knowledge and trust in God is enhanced.

So how can we pursue this one vital relationship? We have our relationships with our children, our relationship with our spouse, we have work, we have pressure, we have so little time and life can lurch from celebration one minute to crisis the next. In the middle of all this, I'm telling you to pursue a relationship with someone you can neither see nor hear. It can sound very difficult and impractical. So how can we pursue a relationship with God? To save us from yet more theory, I think it would be simplest to try to answer this question by meeting one family who succeeded in trusting God in the midst of ordinary life. There is much we can glean from their experience.

MEET THE 'BETHANYS'

I hope that Mary, Martha and Lazarus will forgive me for taking the liberty of loaning them the name of their home town as a surname. I don't know much about biblical surnames beyond 'son of . . .' so, if you would just humour me, I'd like to call them the 'Bethanys', if only to make the point that they were a family. Lazarus, Mary and Martha were brother and sisters. We hear about them in Luke 10:

38–42 and John 11 and 12. Although we only have these two little insights into their home life, it is implied that this is a home where Jesus was a frequent and familiar guest.

Luke starts the story off by telling us about what was possibly the first visit Jesus paid to the home. This episode is recorded in Luke 10:38–42. Lazarus doesn't get a mention in this brief incident but that doesn't mean to say he wasn't there. Luke's attention is drawn to the two sisters, Martha and Mary, whose action and characters seem to contrast so sharply. Mary is quiet, restful and reflective. Martha is busy, bossy and competent. In real life I am sure that they were both far more complex individuals than the rather extreme stereotypes that they have come to assume over the years their story has been retold. Poor Martha! She's had such a bad press, but I really like her. If you take a closer look at her you can see so much more than the rather off-putting first impression. You'll find a woman who does indeed have a growing relationship with Jesus and you can trace the change that this relationship makes in her life.

Let's look at the way Martha comes across when we first meet her in Luke (10:38–42). Jesus is having a meal in the family home and Martha feels that Mary is not doing her fair share of the work so she complains to Jesus, 'Lord don't you care that my sister has left me to do all the work by myself? Tell her to help me!' If ever there was a typical example of demanding anger, this has to be it. Her anger may well be covering up any number of hurt feelings such as jealousy or inadequacy, but instead of taking these hurt feelings to the person concerned, Mary, she goes to complain to a third party, Jesus, and appeals for him to sort out her sister. Ouch! How often have I gone to Jesus in prayer appealing for him to 'sort out the other guy' and he's responded by sorting me out. I have such sympathy for Martha. We have so much in common! Martha is portrayed as the busy, hard-working type. She's decisive, she's self-sufficient, she's well-organised and, yes, let's face it, she's also critical, aggressive and hides her more tender feelings. Whenever you hear someone described today as a 'Martha' the image conjured up is of someone who is good at service but not very spiritual. In this day and age when Christians have largely rejected the Protestant work ethic as 'repressive', spirituality has been elevated above the sheer hard graft of service. Poor Martha is already on her way to a low rating in our culture.

However, whether we like it or not, we parents have to identify ourselves with Martha. Although the presence of children in the home is not mentioned, it does seem clear that Martha had the responsibility for running the home. Notice that it was she who first opened the home to Jesus and welcomed him in (Luke 10:38). I love Martha for just this kind of unconventional directness. Even if her forward nature was the result of being the senior figure in a matriarchal family, at least she used her position well by opening the home up to Jesus. Her directness was of course the same trait that got her into trouble when she came to Jesus to complain about Mary's absence from the kitchen. If we can't identify with Martha for any other reason then surely we must identify with her because of the way that Jesus describes her. What he says could surely be a description of any parent, 'Martha, Martha, you are worried and upset about many things.'

'Too right, I am!' I'd have been tempted to reply. 'Have you seen all the work there is to do in this house? Do you realise how much washing two children can create? Do you realise how many things I *have* to get done today, let alone how many things I'd *like* to have time for?' Before Martha gets to say anything along these lines, Jesus continues, 'Only one thing is needed.' I wonder if he paused for effect at this point? If I'd have been there this would have been the moment when Martha and I would have got out our 'list of things to do' and our pencils and, drumming our fingers impatiently, would have thought, 'Yes, yes, well, tell us what this one thing is, then, and we'll add it to the top of our lists'. Jesus then frustrates us both completely by refusing to tell us explicitly what this 'one necessary thing' is. He points to Mary and implies that she's got 'it' but he doesn't say what 'it' is. Instead, if Martha and I want to find the answer we have to slow down and step back from the scene and think.

Mary has sat at Jesus' feet listening to him. She is clearly hungry to know Jesus better. It is for this that Jesus commends Mary. Luke ends the story at this point, drawing a discreet veil over whatever Martha may, or may not, have said in reply, once she'd had time to think. I know what I'd have been thinking or even saying: 'Yes, Lord, that's all very well and I really would like to be Mary-minded but I happen to have a Martha work-load with the family and kids. What's more it's a work-load you gave me, so what can you expect?'

Jesus' response to this complaint has always been the same: the 'one necessary thing' is not incompatible with a busy schedule or a heavy work-load because the 'one necessary thing' is a relationship with him and a relationship is not something you can tick off your list of things to do today. Because knowing Jesus cannot be easily defined as a task or even a routine, it can seem very unrealistic and impractical to people who are up to their eyes in kids, cooking, cleaning and caring. And yet a relationship is something that develops in the midst of, sometimes in spite of, all the chores and all of life's demands.

I'm sure that Martha must have been initially disheartened by Jesus' rebuke but I think she went away and thought about it. I think she did commit herself to pursuing a relationship with Jesus every bit as much as her sister Mary had done. Evidence for this comes in John 11 where we next meet the family. This time they are in crisis.

Lazarus has fallen ill and together the sisters send word

to Jesus that 'the one whom you love is ill'. The nature of this message leaves us in no doubt that all three members of this family loved Jesus, so it is natural that they turn to him in a crisis. Jesus deliberately waits. His comment that 'this sickness will not end in death' is not the optimistic prognosis that the disciples take it to be. Jesus knew this sickness would result in death but it will not end there. God's greater glory is at stake so Jesus stays put. Our narrator, John, immediately reassures us in the very next verse that Jesus reciprocates the love of this family, lest we should think that his deliberate delay revealed a lack of love and concern. He did love them but he still stood back and waited for their situation to get worse.

When he did finally go to them Lazarus had been dead for four days. Unlike Jairus' daughter who had only been dead for a little while before Jesus came to her, Lazarus is well and truly 'dead and buried'. His friends are four days into their grief when Jesus comes to them. Hearing of his arrival Martha rushes out to meet him on her own. She is not self-conscious, not hanging back assuming he would not be interested or was too important to be bothered with her concerns. Her action seems to me to be the one of someone confident that her feelings would matter to Jesus. She is still just as direct, she still takes the initiative but Jesus does not appear to be at all affronted by her manner nor her questions.

This time Martha has not wasted time talking to a third party about her grievances, this time she brings all her negative feelings to the person concerned, the one she feels has let her down, Jesus. 'Lord . . . if you had been here, my brother would not have died. But I know that even now God will give you whatever you ask.' (John 11:21–22)

Boldly and straight-forwardly, she confronts him with how she feels. Without giving him space to respond to her none-too-veiled criticism she none the less goes on to articulate a stubborn faith that has not died with her brother. Things might seem outwardly hopeless but hope is still alive because of the presence of Jesus.[1]

Jesus listens to her speech, accepting it as completely valid and understandable. He doesn't become defensive or refer to God's greater glory and wider purposes, he speaks directly and straightforwardly. In fact on both sides there is honesty mixed with respect, even though her opening remark could express anything from disappointment to outrage, depending on her tone of voice. Jesus' reply, 'Your brother will rise again', could not have been more specific and direct. But, weary with her grief, Martha assumes that Jesus offers this statement as a conventional comfort and seems to accept that he will rise again on the 'last day'. What a change in Martha! In Luke 10 she tells Jesus how she feels and what he should do about it. This time she simply tells Jesus how she feels, but doesn't tell Jesus what he should do. She has dropped her demand and his comforting presence is enough. She seems willing to accept that the only resurrection for her brother will be on 'the last day'.

Jesus honours this trust with an astounding declaration of truth: 'I am the resurrection and the life. He who believes in me will live, even though he dies; and whoever lives and believes in me will never die' (John 11:25–26). Jesus is saying here that the presence and knowledge of Jesus is the essence of life, eternal life. Death is in fact not the worst thing that can happen to us. The one thing that matters is knowing Jesus and the one who has found life in Jesus cannot die, even though he dies physically, because the knowledge of God is life itself.

'Do you believe this?' Jesus asks Martha and although she has not been able to take up a life of devotion or abandon her work-load she has learnt this, that in the midst of whatever happens it is Jesus who matters most.

She doesn't know how his profound statement is going to affect her own personal situation. She must be wondering what this truth means to her family but when she's asked what she believes she doesn't say, 'I believe you will resurrect my brother'. She doesn't believe Jesus merely for what she hopes he will do, she believes him for who he is: 'Yes Lord, I believe that you are the Christ, the Son of God, who was to come into the world.' Even the very worst that could happen, the death of her brother and presumably the household provider, has not shaken her trust in Jesus. Her ringing declaration of faith, equal to the more often quoted declaration by Peter in Matthew 16:16, is said in the face of uncertainty. Jesus does not hurry to reassure her that her grief will turn to joy, but instead he receives her trust as something of infinite worth. She doesn't yet know or believe that Jesus will restore her brother to life. If she did she would not have any objections to the tomb being re-opened. Her trust is in Jesus not in what she hopes he'll do.

Martha then goes and calls Mary to see Jesus. Mary is clearly a very different character. Not better, or worse, just different. Mary freely expresses her grief, she falls at Jesus' feet sobbing out the same disappointment. Just as Jesus had met Martha in the way that was appropriate for her, he now meets Mary. Martha had come with her honest questions and had been met by a firm declaration of truth. Mary came with her ragged feelings and inarticulate grief and was met with tears of compassion. Mary was in no fit state for a theological conversation – she needed empathy. Maybe during Jesus' delay she had doubted his care for them. His weeping with her was the best reassurance he could have given to her as to the depth of his feeling.

The English words 'deeply moved' cannot really convey the state of inner turmoil that Jesus experienced as he wept. This was no token sympathy. He identified the family's confusion and heart-break in the face of suffering. Even knowing he was about to restore Lazarus to life, he stopped to weep. Maybe he wept for the whole of humanity, living as it does in a fallen world. Maybe he wept for all the suffering that would not be so easily and directly alleviated. Jesus was about to raise Lazarus from the dead but that very action would move Jesus, himself, so much closer to his own death (verse 53). A death that would be the ultimate way of identifying with us in our suffering but also the ultimate way of rescuing us from our suffering. This rescue is effected when we are brought from death to life when we believe in him (John 5:24). There is no guarantee that we shall automatically experience the effects of this rescue (i.e. a life free from pain and hurt) this side of heaven. Why else would Paul have said in Philippians 3:10 that his greatest desire in life was to 'know Christ and the power of his resurrection and the fellowship of sharing in his sufferings'? The pain and the heartache and the imperfection we have to endure as we struggle to bring up our children are all a tiny reflection of the pain and heartache that God feels when he sees his fallen and imperfect world.

Martha's story concludes in John 12 with a celebratory meal which Jesus shares with his three friends. Undoubtedly they have all grown in faith and trust, but we still don't see Mary working in the kitchen or Martha pouring perfume over Jesus' feet. On the contrary it is still Martha who serves and Mary who silently but extravagantly anoints Jesus with perfume. Each sister is affirmed, their worship and service is accepted, they are no longer competitive, one act is not more helpful that the other. Their relationship with Jesus has enhanced rather than changed their natural gifts and characteristics.

Instead of longing to be what we are not, we should seek to allow Jesus to make us more fully at ease with who we are, where we are and what we are. Unless we learn contentment with the talents we have and the place where we've been put and the task he has given us, then we are at risk of focusing on our circumstances and not on Jesus. It is not so much a change in our circumstances that we need but a change in us that causes us to desire that one thing that is needed – a growing awareness of Jesus in our lives as they are now.

HOW DO WE PURSUE A RELATIONSHIP WITH GOD?

If this relationship between you and God is as vital as I've made out then you are likely to be thinking, 'Well, just how do I go about pursuing a relationship with God?' I assume you've discovered how hard it is to maintain this relationship when you are a parent. There is a Spanish proverb which roughly translates as 'The person who really wants to do something will be more successful than the person who merely knows how to do that same thing'. If we apply this proverb to the question 'How do we pursue a relationship with God?' then it is clear that longer devotions, scripture memorisation schemes, greater effort in witnessing are all part of the 'how'. Don't abandon such disciplines but don't think that's all there is to knowing God. Knowing the 'how' isn't enough. The person who really wants to find God is the one who will find him when he seeks God on God's terms. What we need is not a new formula or a new strategy, we need a renewed desire to know God. God has promised that if we really want to find him then we will: 'You will seek me and find me when you seek me with all your heart' (Jeremiah 29:13). Seeking someone with all our heart does not mean with all the emotional energy we can muster. It means without anything else in our heart calling us in another direction. God reveals himself when we whole-heartedly accept him for who he is and when we whole-heartedly trust him and depend on him. This whole-heartedness means there is no room for demands that life runs smoothly, no room for expectations for fulfilment and satisfaction, only room for a hunger for more of God. Whole-heartedness means we are prepared to leave our hopes and fears for ourselves and for our children in the hands of our Heavenly Father. Whole-heartedness says 'I will trust you come what may'.

> I will not doubt, though all my ships at sea come drifting home with broken masts and sails: I shall believe the hand which never fails, from seeming evil worketh good for me. And, though I weep because those sails are battered, still will I cry, while my best hopes lie shattered, 'I trust in thee'.[2]

The hope for the hard-pressed parent lies in coming close to the heart of our loving Heavenly Father with our whole heart. He knows how we feel if our children reject us; he too has experienced that sorrow. He knows our frustration when our children are unruly and disobedient; for he paid the ultimate price for *our* disobedience. He knows how we feel when we give our children the freedom to choose; he gave us that same freedom. The tenderness and compassion that we feel towards our children is only a dim reflection of the tenderness and compassion he feels towards us. Psalm 103 has a lot to tell us about the kind of Father we have in God: 'As a Father has compassion on his children, so the Lord has compassion on those who fear him; for he knows how we are formed, he remembers that we are dust' (v.13).

God is no stranger to what it feels like to be a parent. Nor does he have unrealistic expectations about our ability to parent – 'he knows how we are formed'. He doesn't just understand us, he promises us the strength to love with his own unconditional love, the fruit of his presence in our flawed personalities, the gift of his resources to make up for our meagre abilities. When the daily grind of life gets us down and we feel that all our efforts are meaningless and futile, 'like the flower of the field: the wind blows over it and it is gone, and its place remembers it no more' (v.15), he gives our lives meaning and impact with the astounding promise that 'from everlasting to everlasting the Lord's love is with those who fear him' (v.17). This is not a picture of a Father who is about to abandon us or who might lose interest in us at any moment. Nor is this a picture of a distant, perfect, ideal parent who might make us crumble with a sense of our own inadequacy. Rather here is a picture of our Father who is 'compassionate and gracious, slow to anger, abounding in love' (v.8). He is a close, loving and understanding companion who can guide us through the daily grind, be our friend, be our counsellor and our provider. Above all else, he is on our side.

A Last Word

This book has been written in the midst of family life. I have not waited until I could stand back and benefit from the wisdom and balance afforded by a retrospective view. As a parent I am still at the 'rock-face', so to speak, developing skills and learning as I go. To say I'd mastered anything would be audacious to say the least.

Writing this has made me even more aware of my own imperfections as a parent. I have to apply all the counsel I have offered into my own life. Nor has writing at this stage of our family's life been easy: many a good idea has been chased out of my head by an untimely request for shoes to be tied or stories to be read. I've spent whole mornings trying to recall those good ideas that flew away. I've scribbled down other ideas while waiting at traffic lights, I've written before dawn and into the night. Living several lives within the same four walls (those of wife, mother, writer, friend) has had its hair-raising and hilarious moments. Like the morning when the contract to write this book finally arrived. I left it spread out on the dining room table when a friend called for coffee and my son got his paint pots out while we stood chatting in the kitchen. Only as I admired his third master-piece did I discover that he'd helped himself to the supply of 'scrap-paper' I'd conveniently left lying on the dining room table! It could have qualified as the most colourful legal document in history.

All the stories and anecdotes I have used are true in substance although in places I have changed names and certain details in order to protect privacy. I am deeply grateful to my children for their cheerful good humour in spite of their mother's preoccupied state. Their joyful exuberance has taught me so much. I am also very thankful for my husband David, whose patience and practical help has been essential. My thanks also go to Cathy Hemsley, Alison Morgan and Jonathan Mortimer for their skilful proof-reading and inumerable helpful suggestions. Finally to the many friends in the family of God who have encouraged me, supported me and allowed me to use their stories: thank you for overlooking my imperfections.

Notes

CHAPTER 3: THE PROBLEM IS ME

1. Larry Crabb, *Inside Out* (USA, Navpress 1988)
2. Larry Crabb, *Effective Biblical Counselling* (USA, Zondervan 1977)
3. Susan Lenzkes, *When the Handwriting on the Wall is in Brown Crayon*, © 1981, used with kind permission. (Copies available from 10815 Cascajo Court, San Diego, California 92124)

CHAPTER 4:
FINDING THE PERFECT PARENT IN GOD

1. Angela Ashwin, *Patterns Not Padlocks*, © 1992 Eagle UK

CHAPTER 5: BE YOURSELF

1. *Matthew Henry's Commentary*, Broad Oak Edition (London, Marshall, Morgan and Scott 1960) p. 583
2. Ibid, p. 644

CHAPTER 6: HANDLING THOSE 'HARD-TO-HANDLE' FEELINGS

1. Reg Presley, *Love is all Around*, © 1967 Dick James Music Limited, 47 British Grove, London W4. Used by

permission of Music Sales Limited. All rights reserved. International Copyright Secured.

2. Larry Crabb, Dan Allander, *Encouragement: the Key to Caring* (USA Zondervan 1984)

CHAPTER 7: ANGER:
WHEN YOU FIND YOURSELF SHOUTING

1. Rob Parsons, *Loving Against the Odds* (London, Hodder & Stoughton 1994) p. 22
2. Larry Crabb, *Inside Out* (USA Navpress 1988)

CHAPTER 8: ANGER: TOWARDS BETTER
WAYS OF COMMUNICATION

1. Susan Lenzkes, *Everybody's Breaking Pieces off of Me* (Grand Rapids, Discovery House Publishers 1992)
2. David Augsberger, *Caring Enough to Confront* (UK Marshall Morgan & Scott 1985)
3. Jean Kerr, quoted in *Motherhood: A Gift of Love* (Philadelphia, Running Press 1991)
4. Susan Lenzkes, *When the Handwriting on the Wall is in Brown Crayon* © 1981, used with kind permission.
5. David Augsberger, op. cit. Michael and Terri Quinn, *What Can a Parent Do?* © Family Caring Trust 1989; Ken Blanchard, *The One Minute Manager* (London, HarperCollins 1983)
6. Michael and Terri Quinn, op. cit.
7. Dr Ross Campbell, *How to Really Love your Child* (USA Victor Books 1977) ch. 6.

CHAPTER 9: GUILT:
'MAYBE I'VE DONE THIS ALL WRONG'

1. Melody Beattie, *Co-dependent No More* (Hazelden)

CHAPTER 10: GUILT: 'IF ONLY . . .'

1. Ken Blanchard, *The One Minute Manager* (London, HarperCollins 1983)

CHAPTER 11: ANXIETY:
'YOU CAN'T TEACH CHILDREN ANYTHING'

1. Ken Blanchard, *The One Minute Manager* (London, HarperCollins 1983)
2. Richard Gillard, *The Servant Song* © 1977 Scripture in Song Administered by Copycare Ltd.
3. Joni Earecksantada, *Diamonds in the Dust* (GB 1993 Marshall Pickering)
4. Ulrich Schaeffer from *For the Love of Children* © 1979 Lion Publishing

CHAPTER 12: ANXIETY: CAN I REALLY
TRUST GOD TO LOOK AFTER MY KIDS?

1. C.S. Lewis, *The Problem of Pain*; Philip Yancy, *Where is God when it hurts?* (Marshall Pickering); David Watson, *Fear no Evil* (London, Hodder & Stoughton 1984); *Why us?* Warren Wiersbe, *When Bad Things Happen to God's People* (UK, IVP 1984)

CHAPTER 13: BE NURTURED YOURSELF

1. Rev. Canon Dr Joy Tetley, from *Encounter with God*, April-June 1994, Scripture Union
2. Ella Wheeler Wilcox, quoted in *Draper's Book of Quotations for the Christian World* by Edythe Draper 1992 1

Sun $22 + 2$
cons.

---

since last set
3 likes c dg
over.